CROWBOROUGH'S WAR 1914–1918

PAUL ADAMS

OAK MOSS PUBLICATIONS

First published in 2013 by Oak Moss Publications.
Oak Moss Publications is the publishing imprint of
Adams Real Estate Ltd, 2 Jubilee Cottages, Mardens Hill,
Crowborough TN6 1XW

ISBN 978-0-9926414-0-5

Dedication
This book is dedicated to Nimmy, Len, Oliver, Sid, Jack
& all those from Crowborough & district who served 1914-1918

Typeset & designed by Sue Gent
Lupercaliadesign.com

Printed by CPI Group (UK) CR0 4YY

CONTENTS

INTRODUCTION

In writing this account of Crowborough during the First World War my aim has been to provide an account of what the town was like during the war years, the major events and issues, and how the war impacted the town. I've tried to include as many contemporary photographs as possible, many of which have not been published before. I've also tried to draw on contemporary personal accounts and experiences, including those of my own family, who lived in the St Johns area during the war, and from where my grandfather and his brothers left to serve in the army. Many hundreds of residents of the town served their country in one capacity or another during the war years, and many tens of thousands of troops, British and Canadian, passed through Crowborough Camp - which quickly became a large transit and training facility once the war had started. In addition, troops were billeted in the town, and there was also a military hospital, which treated British, Australian and Canadian troops, and a hospital for wounded Canadian officers. The town also hosted a number of Belgian refugee families, a fact not widely known today.

In choosing the photographs for the book, I'm conscious that postcards - the main source of the illustrations in this book - could have a life span in print over many years, and it is often therefore difficult to date when they were taken precisely. A postmark on the reverse is not necessarily much help. However, I hope that they will help convey an impression of what residents, visitors, and soldiers stationed here would have seen and sensed of the area. We are lucky in that, at the time of the First World War, Crowborough was a major holiday venue, with numerous hotels and guest houses. Because of this popularity, huge numbers

ABOVE: Eridge Road looking north

RIGHT: A group of officers congregating outside a house in Southview Road being used as billets. We know from a message on the reverse of the photo that it was taken in July 1916, and that one of the men present was Second Lieutenant Bannerman of the Queen's Royal West Surrey Regiment. We also know from a report in the local press that the Crowborough Fire Brigade, under Captain Humphry, were called to a kitchen fire at Saffrons in Southview Road, which was also being used to house troops, in April 1915

LEFT: This postcard of Croft Road was sent by a senior officer from Crowborough Camp who was living in a billet in Croft Road in February 1916. He writes; "I am about two miles from the Camp and leave here around 7.30am and return about 5.30pm and lunch in the Camp. My home is in this road... My ration bacon is jolly good." Senior officers like this would have had very little to do with the men under their command. Most basic training would have been undertaken by NCO's and route marches lead by junior officers

of printed and photographic postcards were produced for these visitors to send to friends and family - many of these cards have survived and present us with a detailed picture of the area at that time.

I've also included extracts from many of the messages on the reverse of these postcard images where they have been postally used during the 1914-18 period. In an age still dominated by horse transport and steam trains, postcards were the equivalent of text messages or tweets during this period. Usually brief and informal, and capturing something of the writer's direct experience of a place or event to their friends and families. Whilst it would be impossible to include details of the service of all those in the town who served in the army and other services - a near impossible task which would involve years of research, let alone the vast numbers of soldiers passing through the area, I have included individual stories

ABOVE: Station Road looking towards the town centre

RIGHT: This picture of Pilmer Road reminds us that once you were out of Crowborough Cross you would quickly find yourself in very rustic surroundings

TOP: The Broadway - on the reverse is written; "Just a card of this lovely place" - unknown soldier, Jack, to his sweetheart, February 1915

ABOVE: The lower end of Whitehill Road

and experiences as representative of the generation who served.

Throughout, for the sake of consistency, I refer to Crowborough as "the town". Strictly speaking it was of course a village at the time of the First World War, albeit a rather large and scattered one. Interestingly some contemporary World War One visitors refer to Crowborough as a town. Its population had grown rapidly after the coming of the railway and it had a developed high street with a comprehensive range of shops, so I guess, even then, it did seem more like a town, albeit a very bucolic one, than a village.

Many visitors' idea of a village in those days was probably of a more compact community of a few hundred souls centred on a village green with its pub and one or two shops. Crowborough's resident population at the time, including the St Johns area (all of the St Johns area was officially part of Withyham parish then, but its residents were just as likely to be described as living at Crowborough as Withyham) was very roughly around the 6000 mark (just over 5000 in Crowborough and just under a 1000 in the St Johns area) - very large by the standards of the day for a village.

On another point of nomenclature - the town centre area has traditionally been known as "Crowborough Cross" or "the Cross" - so if someone says they are "going up the Cross" or "to the Cross" it means they are going into town. Contemporary World War One issues of *The Courier* newspaper use the expression in the same way, for example, the Waterloo hut, which stood on the site of the Town Hall, is described in a report as being at Crowborough Cross - even though it is nowhere near the pub (the pub was called the Red Cross Hotel at the time of World War One) or the crossroads. Crowborough's traditional wooden road signs still point to "Crowborough Cross' rather than the "Town Centre".

ABOVE: A verdant looking Whitehill Road captured in a card posted by a visitor to the town in 1918

LEFT: The bucolic nature of Crowborough during the 1914-18 war is evident in this picture of Southview Road

LEFT: Beacon Road and the Blue Anchor pub - note the road stone on the right hand side of the road (the same type of stone can be seen in the photo of Croft Road on page 4) presumably used for making good the road in the pre-asphalt era. This type of road surface didn't cope well with heavy motor vehicle traffic, which created clouds of dust in dry weather and broke up the surface of the road. A great deal of damage was caused to the local roads by the increased military transport during the war years

LEFT: Station Road, Jarvis Brook, looking towards the railway bridge - a familiar sight to the many thousands of troops who arrived in and departed from Crowborough during the war years

The term "the Cross" is therefore traditionally used as a reference to the town centre. Sadly, I've noticed this phrase has been slowly dying out for several decades, under the weight of new residents not familiar with it, coupled with the confusing renaming of the Red Cross Hotel. Now most people say they are going "into town" instead.

In researching this book I have drawn on a number of sources, including contemporary issues of *The Kent & Sussex Courier* newspaper (hereinafter referred to as *The Courier*); and various military records in the National Archives. I have also consulted a number of individuals and organisations who have given generously of their time and knowledge - a full list of acknowledgements can be found at the end of the book.

Growing up as a boy in 1960s Crowborough I was vaguely aware of wartime echoes. There was the Common, with its partially filled in training trenches, which were now just the right height for small boys to use as trenches in war games. And the green cobblers hut in Whitehill where I was often sent on an errand to get some shoes mended (cost always the same - two shillings and sixpence, whatever the repair needed!), which I was told dated from World War One. Then there were the old men, in their flat caps, who used to sit on the benches at Clokes corner on sunny days chatting and watching the world go by - many of whom would have seen First World War service and no doubt have had poignant stories to tell. As I got a bit older, I attended the former drill hall in Fermor Road, which had become the Aldene Youth Club, but which still retained on its walls photos and trophies from its former military users.

BELOW: The Parker Memorial Church in Croft Road was built in 1907 - this postcard was sent by a visitor to the Town in 1915

EVE OF WAR

In the spring of this year (1903) the walls and fences of Crowborough were covered with the placards of a firm of estate agents describing the neighbourhood as 'Scotland in Sussex'. The simile may be true of the Ashdown Forest side of the Beacon, but 'Hampstead in Sussex' would be a more accurate description of Crowborough proper. Never was a fine remote hill so be-villa'd The east slope is all scaffold poles and heaps of bricks, new churches and chapels are sprouting, and many hoardings announce that Follies, Pierrots, or conjurers are continually imminent. Crowborough itself has shops that would not disgrace Croydon, and a hotel where a Lord Mayor might feel at home. Houses in their own grounds are commoner than cottages, and near the summit the pegs of ***surveyors and the name-boards of avenues yet to be built testify*** *to the charms which our Saxon Caledonia has already exerted.*

Extract from *Highways and Byways in Sussex* by E.V. Lucas, 1904

TOP: The golf club with a distant view of the South Downs

ABOVE: A pre-war picnic party enjoying a view of the mill pond - the pond and mill building were a magnet for middle class visitors to Crowborough in the carefree summers before the war

RURAL IDYLL

You only have to glance at old photos or read contemporary accounts to realise what a charming place Crowborough must have been in 1914, even though some writers of the time, like Lucas, were already concerned that it was becoming too suburban and populous. It had expanded rapidly over the previous 40 years, but still retained an idyllic air. This, coupled with its promotion as a health resort by Dr Leeson Prince in the Victorian period, was responsible for its rosy reputation as a place to live or visit.

This boom in middle class residents and visitors meant that the local economy could support numerous shops, small family farms and building firms, as well as brick works - the largest being at Jarvis Brook - and small sandstone quarries which supplied materials for the new houses being built. One of the biggest employment growth areas was horticulture, due to the demand from the hotels and guest houses for bulk supplies of vegetables and fruit. Crowborough-grown tomatoes are said to have had a particularly fine reputation in the district. Amidst this economic growth and prosperity we mustn't forget though that, among working people, there was a considerable amount of poverty and deprivation as well.

The jewels in Crowborough's crown at the time were undoubtedly its large hotels. The most impressive of these was the Beacon Hotel - this large establishment must have provided a huge amount of employment in its heyday, both in terms of the staff it employed, as well as by its spending on local goods and services. Of course its guests' spending power would have also boosted the local economy.

Crowborough's local cottage hospital has its origins in the early 1900's when the District Nursing Association took a lease on a property, Preston Lodge, in Southview Road, as the accommodation it

TOP LEFT: An arcadian looking London Road

BOTTOM LEFT: The author's great grandfather, Abraham, working in a local hop garden

ABOVE AND LEFT: The Beacon Hotel - Crowborough boasted a number of large hotels and several smaller ones at the time of the First World War

LEFT: Guests at the Beacon Hotel play croquet on the lawn as the storm clouds gather in Europe

RIGHT: Whitehill School was built as a school for juniors and infants and opened in April 1894. A further classroom was added in 1897. A separate infants' school was completed at the rear of the existing building in 1900. Further improvements were made to the building including an extension in 1909. The school continued in use for juniors and infants until 1967 when Herne County Primary School was built in Herne Road and the juniors were transferred

had previously occupied in the same area was proving inadequate. During the First World War therefore the nucleus of the present hospital already existed. Also in the years before the war Crowborough's most famous resident, Arthur Conan Doyle, had settled in the town. Crowborough even had its very own Building Society - the Crowborough and District Mutual Building Society - which had been formed in the Edwardian era.

RIGHT: Whitehill Road

BELOW: A bustling Crowborough station - with a nice coal fire to warm travellers up in the waiting room no doubt

ST JOHNS COMMON

The Crowborough district was no stranger to military activities in the Edwardian era. In particular, St Johns Common usually hosted some kind of large military camp during the July-August period each year. In July 1908, for example, 60 officers and 600 men of the 12th, 20th and 23rd Brigades of the Royal Field Artillery camped on the common, training for manoeuvres in the New Forest. They arrived on a Saturday and many of them went to a service at St Johns Church the next morning. In July 1912 an even bigger camp was held by several units which arrived by a series of special trains at Crowborough station.
These camps naturally attracted sightseers from the district, including the many people who holidayed in the area at this time of the year. At this time, my paternal grandfather and his family lived

ABOVE: This charming photo, taken during the Royal Field Artillery camp of 1908, shows a group of Royal Artillery Drivers on St Johns Common, returning to their lines having just watered their horses at the mill pond. The top of the mill building can just be seen nestling among the trees in the background, between the heads of the two leading horsemen

LEFT: In this photo, taken from near Friars Gate and looking towards St Johns Common, we can just see the white tents of a pre-war Territorial Force summer camp on the Common in the middle horizon

RIGHT: This postcard gives a better glimpse than most of the layout of the mill buildings complex , it was sent by a soldier on the Territorial Force summer camp on St Johns common in 1911. He observes; "Crowborough a very scattered place - miles between each part. No water for washing or drinking until after tea today in our lines. Short everywhere, but especially so with us as we are at the end of pipe from Crowborough..."

BELOW: Another photo of one of the massive pre-war TF camps on St Johns Common

ABOVE: London Territorial Force soldiers, helped by a young lad, make themselves at home on St Johns Common for their annual summer camp from 28th July to 11th August 1912. The boy is likely to be visiting the area on holiday (Crowborough was a major tourist attraction in the Edwardian Era, with several large hotels, and numerous smaller ones) as he looks too well dressed to be a local farmworker's son. St Johns Common, with its mill building and mill ponds, was a magnet for visitors. In the summer Mrs Avis, who lived in a cottage next to the mill, provided cream teas for visitors

LEFT: This photo shows the extent of the 1912 Territorial Force summer camp on St Johns Common. The TF paid the conservators of the Ashdown Forest £4 for the use of the Common. Some 1400 men and 800 horses were present, arriving in Crowborough in a series of special trains. The sender of this postcard notes; "Have had to dig trenches all round tents today, flooded out". Contemporary reports in *The Courier* describe the weather as "wet and boisterous" for much of their stay

in a cottage across the track from the New Mill. In another cottage near the mill dam lived Mrs Avis. She provided cream teas for visitors during the summer - the mill pond and surrounding area was a well known beauty spot, with well worn paths leading from the common down to the mill, where people often picnicked. At this time the huge water wheel on the mill was still in place - it was apparently cut up and taken away as scrap metal during the Second World War.

My paternal grandmother's family also lived in the St Johns area, and both my grandmother and grandfather attended St Johns School. The school leaving age then was 14, so my grandfather would have

FAR LEFT: St Johns Church has changed very little in the last 100 years, although the demographic of the community it serves has changed immensely

ABOVE: Lower St Johns Road looking like the country lane it then was

RIGHT: Coopers Lane, narrower than today, but the Coopers Arms is much the same

RIGHT: The top part of St Johns Road looks familiar

LEFT AND ABOVE:
Postcards showing the junction of School Lane with St Johns Road. Today there is a phone box and a rare Edward V111 post box where the roads meet. The house shown left is still there, presumably replacing the more modest sandstone cottage shown above. What is now the St Johns car park appears to have been a stone quarry

left school around 1908 I would think. My grandmother would have still been a scholar during the war years, and, in fact, in trawling through the old issues of *The Courier* newspaper, I came across a reference to her in 1915 - when she not only won a school award for her needlework, but also an honour prize for being; "the best conducted girl in her class". Local newspapers are a mine of useful historical information, and we all owe a great debt to *The Kent & Sussex Courier* for its meticulous reporting of local goings on all those years ago.

The St Johns area included some of the poorest parts of the Crowborough district at the time of the First World War. In the early 1900s some children from St Johns were said to go barefoot in summer because their parents were so poor. At the end of the school summer holidays the children were often allowed extra days off school to help with the hop picking. The money earned would usually go towards a pair of boots for the winter.

Various tiny charities had been set up by philanthropic benefactors to help the local "deserving poor". Often these charities would dispense what, even by the standards of the day, could be regarded as very basic and limited help. In January 1917, for instance, the Thomas Moorhouse charity made its annual distribution of loaves of bread for the deserving poor residing on the Lye Green side of Withyham parish.

ABOVE: Forest Fold Baptist Chapel with its pastor, Ebenezer Littleton

LEFT: Hop growing was still an important part of local rural life at the time of the First World War. Unlike many parts of Kent where working class Londoners did much of the picking, most hop gardens in the fields around Crowborough were picked by poor local people, the seasonal work giving a welcome boost to family finances, and often helping to pay for new boots for the children ahead of the start of the school year

By this time wartime food price inflation, caused by the German U Boat campaign, meant that its endowment could only purchase a considerably reduced number of loaves. According to a report in *The Courier* newspaper; "The Trustees spent a great deal of their time making a judicious allotment of the 297 loaves at their disposal". The charity was still going in 1919 when the Trustees managed to distribute 312 loaves among 127 families. You wonder how these families managed for bread for the rest of the year.

It is quite touching that, despite the poverty in the St Johns area, a number of fund-raising events were held during the war by the local school children in aid of refugee and service charities. In December 1916, for instance, the school gave a concert in aid of the Blind Soldiers' Fund. This help mirrored the very generous fund raising undertaken throughout Crowborough for war related good causes and "comforts for the troops".

LEFT: Territorial Force (TF) soldiers under canvas at Crowborough. The TF of part-time soldiers (the precursors of today's Territorial Army) was formed in 1908. Territorial Force units initially saw service in Egypt, India and other Empire garrisons such as Gibraltar, thereby releasing regular units for service in France and enabling the formation of an additional five regular army divisions by early 1915. The man in the centre at the bottom of the photo is wearing the Imperial Service badge over his right breast pocket, indicating that he has volunteered to serve overseas

WAR IS DECLARED

In 1914 many visitors spent their summer holidays in Crowborough as usual. However, when war was declared by Britain on Germany on August 4th, the usual influx was curtailed by the "gravity of national affairs", according to *The Courier*. The paper went on to report; "The hotels have been somewhat handicapped by the departure of foreign waiters...some have however returned to their duties, being unable to get through to their (home) countries."

LEFT: Camps were set up at Crowborough soon after the start of the war. This photo was taken in September 1914. The soldier who sent this card writes; "This is our camp... we are having rough weather, raining every day. I am on the sick list with blistered feet after 23 mile march."

ABOVE: This photo shows the 1/8th City of London Battalion of the London Regiment (Post Office Rifles) who arrived at Crowborough in September 1914. This postcard sent in October, shows them on a route march on the Forest, probably between Crowborough and Nutley. The unit, which comprised mostly Post Office employees, landed in France in March 1915

At a meeting at the Oddfellows Hall on 7th August 1914, a few days after war had been declared, Sir Arthur Conan Doyle made a very prescient speech. He commented; "We are standing at a critical moment of our lives...after this war things will never be quite the same again."

At the same time, *The Courier* was reporting that the local boy scouts, under their scoutmaster, Mr Southon, were anxious to do their bit. According to the report Mr Southon was; "busy making arrangements for the placing of the boys in connection with the general plan of the (Scouting) Association." What this plan was is not known, but we do know that it was envisaged that the Scouts would be involved in a civil defence role during the war, though surviving reports of their actual wartime activities are few and far between.

Very early on in the conflict it was decided that Crowborough would be a good place to station troops. The possibility of finding billets for troops was mooted, and plans were made for permanent camps to be established at St Johns Common and in the "Crow & Gate district". The camp that developed in the "Crow & Gate district", at Brown Knoll, which

ABOVE: A view from the railway bridge in Jarvis Brook showing St Michael & All Angels church. The church, built in 1905, would have been a familiar sight to troops marching from the railway station to Crowborough Camp

became the Warren Camp, was eventually to become a very significant hutted site.

Such was the influx of troops that on 25th September the local magistrates, presumably fearing an outbreak of drunken disorder, decided to order all public houses in Crowborough to close at 9.00pm each night; "due to the large number of troops encamped in the immediate district."

In October, the Clerk to Crowborough parish council was asked to; "Draw the attention of the Uckfield Rural District Council to the damage being done to the Crowborough roads by the extraordinary traffic caused by the military authorities and their contractors."

"Thank you for your letter and the tobacco which arrived this morning. Lovely country round here. In the field where we are now there are about 30 tents, 6 wagons and 20 horses tied up." Private Baker, Crowborough, letter to his sister 10th November 1914.

"We are getting plenty of wind and rain and our camp is ankle deep in mud, but I am feeling very fit, never felt better. This last two days we have been turf cutting and building the mounds for our range, which is about four miles from the camp. I think our company go through their course of firing tomorrow." Junior officer, Crowborough, to his sister 3rd December 1914.

War had been declared in late summer, and although initially, as elsewhere in the country, men had been accommodated under canvas, as winter approached there was a massive hut building programme at newly established camps all over the country. Towards the end of November 1914, *The Courier* was able to report that; "The (tented) camp at St Johns is now almost deserted, and the few men left are to be transferred to the huts at Little Warren Farm (Brown Knoll)."

Despite all the hut building however, tents continued to be used, probably as supplementary accommodation during the warmer months, throughout the war - for instance, in May 1918 *The Courier* carried a report about an inquest into the death of a soldier at Crowborough "who died in his tent".

WHO'S ABSENT?
Is it You?

CROWBOROUGH'S MEN JOIN UP

At the outbreak of the war, the British Army was a professional force of some 247,000 men, half of which was stationed overseas in the outposts of Empire. It was a small force in comparison with many continental European armies of the time. It was supported by its reservists (trained and ex-soldiers re-called from civilian life) and by 269,000 Territorial Force (TF) soldiers. The TF (forerunners of today's Territorial Army) were part time soldiers, who trained in their spare time.

THE CINQUE PORTS BATTALION

The TF unit whose recruiting area covered Crowborough was the 5th (Cinque Ports) Battalion of the Royal Sussex Regiment. Its local contingent, G Company, comprising some 100 men, mostly local farm labourers, builders' labourers and domestic employees, met regularly at a hut in Whitehill Road (thought to be on the site of the present Scout building). In February 1914 their new purpose built brick hall was completed in Fermor Road and officially opened by Sir Arthur Conan Doyle. It was a well-appointed building with offices and a range as well as a hall for drilling.

The Hall was built by Uckfield "builder and house furnisher" Alfred Chilton at a cost of £1200, on land donated to the Sussex Territorial Force Association by "Mr Troy" - probably William Troy, a retired farmer. The furnishings were supplied by Whitehill furniture dealer Albert Houghton at a cost of about £50.

Recruits joined the TF for periods of **four years, attending** regular meetings at the local company drill hall, as well as a two week annual summer camp with the whole of their battalion (some 600-800

ABOVE: Soldiers mill about at Crowborough Cross

OPPOSITE: The Parliamentary Recruiting Committee oversaw the production of over 50 million copies of some 200 different recruiting posters during the war. This one features an iconic John Bull pointing an accusatory finger

ABOVE: A soldier, identity unknown, on horseback outside Frances Goodacre's tobacconist shop on the corner of Croham Road. The shop is now a solicitor's office, and most of the building has changed very little. Mrs Goodacre's son, Arthur, who was a gardener in civilian life, went to France with the 2nd Battalion Royal Sussex Regiment in January 1915. He was killed in action in September of the same year. In a doubling of the tragedy, another of Mrs Goodacre's sons, Frederick, was killed two years later, in 1917, whilst serving with the Ox & Bucks Light Infantry – both sons were aged 19 when they died

RIGHT: Sussex Yeomanry cap badge

RIGHT: Royal Sussex Regiment cap badge

men) usually held between late July and mid August. The annual summer camp in particular was popular, as it gave ordinary working men who would not normally have had holidays the chance for a break from their usual routine.

Although the TF was originally envisaged as a home defence force it was quickly appreciated that it could help bolster the army in France, both directly, by TF units being sent to France, and indirectly, by TF units being sent to relieve regular troops garrisoned in the Empire, who would then be freed up for service in Europe. After a spell guarding the Tower of London in January 1915, local G Company men were welcomed back to Crowborough on 22nd January 1915. Most of them then proceeded to France with their Battalion in February 1915.

Territorial Force men who volunteered to serve overseas were awarded a special "Imperial Service" badge to wear over the

right breast pocket of their tunic. Home service TF men were drafted to "Provisional Battalions" which were mainly used to man the east coast defences and the Thames estuary - places seen as most likely spots for German raids and landings.

SUSSEX YEOMANRY

The Sussex Yeomanry was the local cavalry component of the TF. Formed in 1908, it had its headquarters at Brighton. Its Lewes squadron recruiting area covered Eridge, Uckfield and Tunbridge Wells - so it is likely that some men who preferred a mounted role rather than an infantry one in the Crowborough district would have joined this unit. It is known that there was quite a large Crowborough contingent in the Sussex Yeomanry cadets local company during the latter part of the war. The Sussex Yeomanry fought dismounted at Gallipoli and elsewhere in the Middle East, ending up in an infantry role in France in 1918.

KITCHENER'S ARMY

In 1914, soon after the start of the war, a new force came into being. At the start of the war, Lord Kitchener became Secretary of State for War, a member of the Government. One of the few to foresee a long war, he was sceptical of the TF, with its home service ethos, and he wanted to organise a new force outside of their framework to supplement the regular army. The result, called the New Army, was the largest volunteer army that Britain had seen. Kitchener's commanding image, appearing on recruiting posters demanding "Your country needs you!", is still a powerful image today. When we see First World War photos of men enthusiastically queuing up to join the army in the early months of the war, it is generally the New Army, or "Kitchener's Army" as it was known popularly at the time, that they were queuing to join. Almost 2.5 million men volunteered for Kitchener's Army between 1914 and the introduction of conscription in 1916.

ABOVE: Chapel Green has been the venue for many of Crowborough's important celebrations and events over the last 100 years

ABOVE: Cinque Ports Battalion button

ABOVE: John (Jack) Tasker shortly after joining up. An early port of call for most new Crowborough recruits was Stickells photography shop in Croft Road, where they would have a portrait photo taken for friends, family and sweethearts

ABOVE RIGHT: Jack Tasker a couple of years later with his wife Emily. Now a veteran soldier he has a good conduct chevron on his lower left sleeve. The two slender stripes below this are wound stripes, indicating that he has been wounded in action twice by the time this later picture was taken. Photographers always ensured that wound stripes were visible in any portrait pictures they took

TERRITORIAL FORCE EXPANDS

Whilst this augmentation of the regular army was taking place, the Territorial Force was also being considerably increased. A second battalion of the 5th Cinque Ports was formed in November 1914, known as the 2/5th (Cinque Ports) Battalion Royal Sussex Regiment. By February 1915 just under 400 local men were thought to be serving in the various branches of HM Armed Forces. At his High Street recruiting office, the Crowborough honorary recruiting officer, Mr Hardwicke, was doing brisk business issuing "warrants" to new recruits - presumably to cover their train passage to a recruiting depot.

SERVICE RECORDS

Unfortunately, many individual wartime service records from the First World War were lost during the Blitz in the Second World War. Some of the records that have survived were damaged by fire or water. However, it is clear from those records that survive, that, around this time (November 1914), a number of local Crowborough men joined this new battalion of the Territorial Force. In joining the TF they were agreeing to serve in home defence, unless they specifically opted to sign the "Imperial Service Obligation" which meant they could be sent overseas if required. When conscription was introduced in 1916, any fit home service Territorials automatically became available for overseas service.

It is a common misconception that men nearly always joined their local county regiment. County regiments often recruited outside of their County boundaries. Throughout the war a cachet was attached to serving with the regular 1st and 2nd Battalions of an infantry regiment, or with Guards or cavalry Regiments, and some men signed on as regulars rather than for four years with the Territorials or "for the duration of the war" with Kitchener's Army. Once in the Army, men were frequently posted to other units anyway, so that over the course of the war it was not uncommon for 'old sweats' to see service with three or four different regiments or corps. Younger men, who generally recovered better from illness and wounds, might spend their whole war in the infantry. But older men, in their thirties and forties, who had started off in the infantry often finished their service in the Labour Corps or other non-front line units if their medical fitness category had been reduced by illness or wounds.

When conscription was introduced in 1916, although, in theory there was scope for men to express a preference for which regiment or corps they wished to join, in practice they were posted to a unit of the Army's choosing - if they were a fit young man that usually meant to an infantry regiment where they were very likely to see front line service.

However, if they were less physically capable, or they were a skilled tradesman of some sort, they might be sent to a behind the lines support unit, or even be kept at home and be posted to a base unit or an agricultural unit. Territorial Force soldiers had generally been promised when they had joined up that they would serve with their own units. However the exigencies of war meant that the Army Council needed greater flexibility in allocating manpower than this allowed for. The military authorities therefore announced that; "The wastage of this war makes it desirable that the Army Council should be enabled to liquify its assets, and to make such transfers as will secure the best distribution in the field."

These "transfers" could mean that men saw service with several different regiments during the course of the war. Even if they stayed within their regiment, they could be transferred about between that regiment's various battalions. Pre-war, most infantry regiments had two regular battalions, plus a reserve battalion, made up of ex-soldiers and

ABOVE: Sam Heasman of Friars Gate (right) in his Army Service Corps uniform. The seated man next to him appears in a number of other Heasman family photos and is thought to be a family member or friend. His cap badge looks like that of the 10th Hussars or 3rd Dragoons

LEFT: Imperial Service Badge - this was awarded to Territorial Force men who volunteered for overseas service

special reservists called up in time of war, and a TF battalion. During the war most infantry regiments expanded exponentially - the Royal Sussex Regiment ended up with 26 Battalions (there were around 800-900 men in a full strength battalion). Some other regiments expanded even more - the Northumberland Fusiliers had 51 battalions by the war's end.

A good example of inter-battalion transfer is the case of local man Private Percy Chandler. Private Chandler served in no less than five different battalions of the Royal Sussex Regiment in France between August 1916 and his capture by the Germans in March 1918 while serving with

RIGHT: The violation of Belgian neutrality by the German Army was used as a popular rallying cry by the British Government early in the war

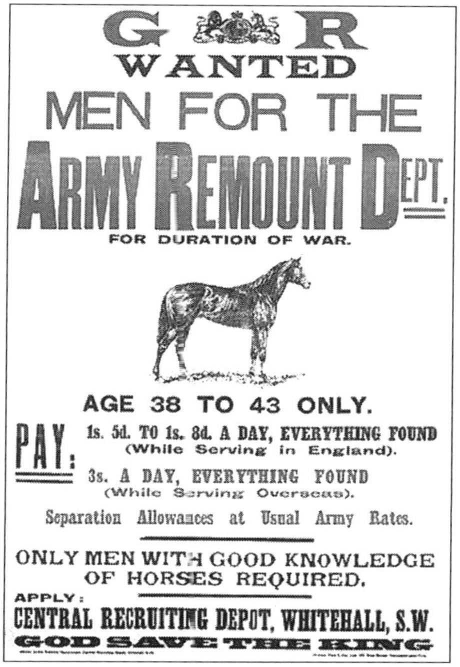

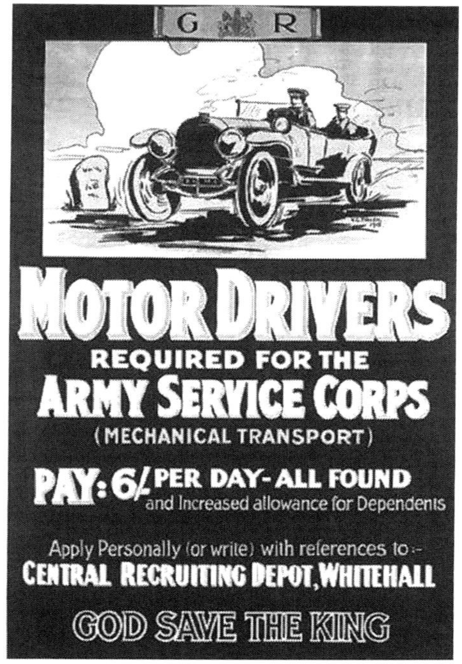

LEFT: The military was keen to recruit men with specialist skills or know-how. Enhanced rates of pay were offered, often several times the pay of an infantryman. Crowborough's relatively numerous chaffeurs and taxi drivers were particularly sought after by the Army Service Corps

FAR LEFT: Men with equine experience were also in demand for an army still very reliant on horsepower. At the beginning of the War the Army owned 25000 horses; tens of thousands more were recruited in the first few weeks of the conflict alone

the regiment's 4th battalion. He was finally repatriated by the Germans in early 1919.

Diversity of recruitment and postings was a good thing - communities with "Pals Battalions" could (and many did) have practically all their able-bodied male population taken from them in single actions. The Pals Battalions were locally recruited units from individual towns (some 50 towns had formed these battalions by September 1914) - the idea being that men were more likely to join up if they were promised they could fight alongside their friends and neighbours.

Crowborough was not big enough to be part of the "Pals Battalions" movement, though of course there was a contingent of local men in the Cinque Ports Battalion and, later on, after conscription was introduced, in the new South Down Battalions of the Royal Sussex Regiment, and the latter suffered heavy casualties in the Battle of the Somme. By the time conscription was introduced the authorities had realised that, although as a recruiting strategy Pals Battalions had been very successful, congregating men from a limited catchment area together in one unit, which could suffer heavy casualties, was bad for home front morale and the cohesion of the community affected if the worst happened. The practice was therefore dropped.

UNDERAGE RECRUITS

The early war phenomenon of underage boys enlisting is well-known. When joining up as a volunteer in 1914 or 1915 the recruit made a statement as to their age, and, if they stated their age as being 18 or over, they weren't required to back this up with any evidence, such as a birth certificate. Crowborough was not without its fair share of youthful underage volunteers and a number of cases are known.

A common belief today is that the Army actively recruited boys to send off off to war. In fact, looking through the surviving records of Crowborough soldiers creates a different impression. From a number of local records I have examined under age boys were usually weeded out within a month or so by the Army and discharged. An example was

[Form to be used when the whole of the Army Reserve is called out.]

GENERAL MOBILIZATION

Army Reserve

(REGULAR AND SPECIAL RESERVISTS).

HIS MAJESTY THE KING has been graciously pleased to direct by Proclamation that the Army Reserve be called out on permanent service.

ALL REGULAR RESERVISTS are required to report themselves at once at their place of joining in accordance with the instructions on their identity certificates for the purpose of joining the Army.

ALL SPECIAL RESERVISTS are required to report themselves on such date and at such places as they may be directed to attend for the purpose of joining the Army. If they have not received any such directions, or if they have changed their address since last attendance at drill or training, they will report themselves at once, by letter, to the Adjutant of their Unit or Depot.

The necessary instructions as to their joining will then be given.

RIGHT: A poster proclaiming the mobilisation of the Army Reserve. Regular reservists were time served ex-soldiers liable for recall, and special reservists were civilians who had undergone six months of military training before returning to their civilian occupation on the understanding that they would be called up in time of war

young George Groombridge, who travelled from Crowborough to a London recruiting office in September 1914 and joined the Yorkshire Light Infantry - he was probably aged about 14, but managed to pass himself off as 18. He remained in the army for 41 days before being discharged; "having made a misstatement as to age on enlistment" according to surviving records in the National Archives.

An odder case concerns another 14 year calling himself "John Smith". This lad, claiming to be from Crowborough and aged 19, was in fact a Londoner called John Connor. He joined the London Regiment and managed to serve for 245 days before his parents found his whereabouts and wrote to his Commanding Officer, providing him with a copy of the boy's birth certificate showing his real name and age and requesting his discharge. Why this boy chose to give his home address as Crowborough is unclear. He is said to have run away from home before he joined up, so possibly he spent some time in Crowborough before he joined the Army. There were obviously cases that slipped through the net - a stout, tall youth might well be able to pass himself off as older than he really was, especially given that the average height of working men then tended to be lower than today, due to a more restricted diet. But the Army doesn't seemed to have turned a blind eye if evidence came to light of a recruit's real age - at least in the local cases I came across. Estimates vary widely as to the scale of the phenomenon nationally, but have been revised down in recent years.

LEGITIMATE YOUNG SOLDIERS

Another point to remember is that there were plenty of legitimate ways for boys to join the army - albeit with less pay, and less chance of overseas service. The practice of boy soldiers joining the regular army in a non-combatant role continued during the war years. These lads generally joined as drummer boys or buglers, and usually served in the UK in their regiment's home depot. One such example is John Izzard of Gladstone Road. He enlisted "for the duration of the war" as a boy soldier aged 15 years and 6 months in January 1918, under a scheme to free up adult TF soldiers for other duties, and served as a drummer boy with the Northamptonshire Regiment. His parents, like those of other legitimate non-combatant boy soldiers, had to sign a consent form to enable him to join, and, unlike recruits claiming to be 18 plus, a birth certificate would have had to have been produced. Boys enlisting into an infantry battalion as drummers, buglers or pipers between the ages of 15 and 17.5 years were paid 8d a day. On reaching the age of 18 they would have been fully trained in all infantry duties and officially become liable for drafting overseas at the age of 19 (later reduced to 18).

The TF could recruit men aged from 17 years old. Nelson Pilbeam, a gardener from Southview, joined the 5th Cinque Ports battalion on 7th August 1914 aged 17 years and 7 months. He was sent to France in February 1915, when he would have just turned 18 - this would have been when the official age for overseas service was still 19, showing that there was some latitude in the rules. He was wounded in action in August (he suffered a gunshot wound to his thigh) when he would have been just over 18 and a half.

The introduction of conscription in 1916 meant that the scope for overstating, or, in the case of older would-be soldiers, understating, your age wasn't such an issue, as the whole process became much more bureaucratic and men waited to be called up.

LARGE FAMILIES

Many local working people had large families in this era - 13, 14 or more children was not uncommon. Many parents therefore found themselves with several sons of military age. My great-grandparents had five sons who served, but this was quite a modest number compared to some. For example, William and Mary Boarer, who ran the Old Half Moon pub at Friar's Gate, had eight sons who served (two of whom died). One, Private Walter Boarer, who lived at Western Road, and who was called up in February 1917, was posted to France in May 1917 and won the Military Medal for gallantry in the field in October. Sadly, Walter died of wounds in June 1918. He left a wife and two young children.

SERVICE OVERSEAS

Not very many men, relative to the several million from the UK who served during World War One, spent the entire four years of the war in France. One such Crowborough man who did was 21 year old waiter Harold Arnold. Harold had joined the Army's special reserve in 1911. This meant that he had undergone six months full-time military training before returning to civilian life, but was able to be recalled in time of war. On the outbreak of war he was called up and joined the British Expeditionary Force (BEF), as the British Army in France and Flanders was known, on 22nd August 1914. Apart from a few periods of leave in the UK amounting to a couple of months in total, he wasn't finally sent home until 13th January 1919 - a total of 4 years and 145 days later.

Most men who joined up in 1914, in the great recruitment drive after the war was declared, didn't start arriving in France until early 1915, having undergone the relevant training. In the first few months of the war it was the regular army, supported by recalled reservists and special reservists like Harold Arnold, who shouldered most of the fighting. It was these men who proudly styled themselves the "Old Contemptibles" in reference to the Kaiser's dismissive remarks about Britain's small peace-time Army.

ABOVE: The role of women as sweethearts, sisters and mothers was given great prominence during the war - this popular wartime postcard was one of numerous cards produced on this theme

The War of 1914-1918.

Royal Garrison Artillery

34644 Gnr. O. Mackellow, 131st Hy. By.

was mentioned in a Despatch from

Major General A. R. Hoskins. C.M.G., D.S.O.

dated 30th May 1917

for gallant and distinguished services in the Field.

I have it in command from the King to record His Majesty's high appreciation of the services rendered.

Winston S. Churchill

Secretary of State for War.

War Office
Whitehall S.W.
1st March 1919.

LEFT: Oscar Mackellow. He is wearing a Cinque Ports Battalion cap badge. His collar badges are brass pioneers badges in the form of a crossed rifle and pick on each collar. This dates the picture to after 20th August 1915, as that is when the Cinque Ports Battalion was made the pioneer battalion of the 48th (South Midland) Division. His service records do not appear to survive in the National Archives, but his medal index card suggests he went to France after the end of 1915, probably in a draft of replacements. We know he served overseas with the Royal Artillery with whom he was mentioned in despatches in May 1917 for "gallant and distinguished services in the field."

ABOVE AND OPPOSITE: Views of Mardens Hill which are easily recognisable today, with the then unspoiled Jubilee Cottages in the foreground of the picture opposite. Mardens Hill is often spelt Marden Hill on postcards of the time

MOTOR DRIVERS

In order to understand the various roles local men played in the conflict it is useful to understand something of the local economy at the time. A good example is that of chauffeurs and taxi drivers. Crowborough was a tourist destination of some note at the time of the First World War. It had several large and numerous smaller hotels and guest houses. In addition it was a popular home for the minor gentry and those of independent means. This meant, among other things, that there was quite a good sprinkling of chauffeurs and taxi drivers among the local male population. These men soon found themselves in great demand by the Motor Transport section of the Army Service Corps. The Army Service Corps Motor Transport branch was headquartered at Grove Park in London, and several local men with motor driving experience joined up there. Such was the demand for drivers, they were often posted to France within weeks of joining.

RESERVES

Not every man who volunteered or, after 1916, was conscripted, found themselves posted to a military unit. It was not uncommon for enlisted men to be immediately posted to the army reserves. This meant they continued in civilian life until they were "mobilised", which might not happen for weeks, months or, in a few cases, years. Such men usually had a skill or trade that meant they were deemed to be more useful to the war effort as a civilian. In the industrial heartlands of England, this might mean they were skilled machinists, engineers or metal workers. In Crowborough this could mean bricklayers or carpenters. If and when these men were mobilised they would often be posted to a unit such as the Royal Engineers where their civilian skills could be put to best use.

ALLOCATION

In fact the Army was a very efficient manpower sifting operation. Men were

directed to where they could be most useful. Occasionally men in uniform were transferred to the army reserve to enable them to return to their civilian occupation. Farm labourers who worked with animals might find themselves posted to the Army Veterinary Corps, general farm workers might find themselves posted to an agricultural labour unit.

An interesting example of men being directed to where they could be most useful is that of G. H. Paynter, a Crowborough parish councillor who was called up in late 1917. Mr Paynter was; "well-known in the pigeon world" according to *The Courier*. On enlistment he was therefore posted to the Army Pigeon Service, a branch of the Royal Engineers. Homing pigeons actually played an important role in communicating messages during the war. They were specifically protected under the Defence of the Realm regulations. Anyone who "killed, wounded or molested" homing pigeons faced a £100 fine, and a £5 reward was offered for information securing the conviction of anyone; "killing or concealing naval or military carrier pigeons."

After 1916, local conscripts would report to a recruiting office in Sussex when they were called up (usually Chichester), but they would find themselves posted to where their level of fitness, and type of skills they possessed, made them most suitable - this could be any corps or county regiment of the British Army - though local men posted to the infantry seem to have been sent to English county regiments. I haven't come across anyone in the surviving records that I sampled that was posted to a Scottish, Welsh or Irish regiment. The average Crowborough recruit's regiment's "home depot" could be a long way away from Crowborough.

MANPOWER SHORTAGES

Conscription was introduced early in 1916, originally for single men aged 18 to 41. The

RIGHT: This card of Mardens Hill was posted in May 1916 by 21 year old Trooper George Gowin of the 3/1st Royal East Kent Mounted Rifles. Trooper Gowin's unit moved to Crowborough Camp around that time. He notes on his card; "We shifted today (from Crowborough Camp). We are (now) camped in the woods miles from anywhere". He is probably referring to St Johns Common, which seems to have been used as additional accommodation for troops from the main camp at times during the war, especially in the summer months. He probably chose this postcard as representing a view he'd seen. He goes on to say; "I think there's an order being put through to keep us as cavalry" In fact his unit was disbanded early in 1917, its personnel becoming infantrymen. Trooper Gowin hailed from North Marston, Buckinghamshire, and, according to the 1911 census he was a "grocer's errand boy". His younger brother Ernest joined the Navy in 1915 and was killed in action in February 1917 whilst serving as an infantryman with the Royal Naval Division in France

law went through several changes before the war ended. Married men were soon included, and the age limit was raised. As the war wore on recognition of work of national importance diminished as a reason for men not to be mobilised, owing to the desperate need for more manpower in the Army. In the final year of the war several local men well into their late 40s were called up. Elsewhere I have come across examples of even older men being enlisted as Privates - one Canadian I came across in my research who joined the Royal Engineers was over 60 on enlistment!

MEDICAL CATEGORIES

The Army usually recognised that these older men were not suitable for front line duties. One local man, a gardener, called up aged 45 years and 8 months in August 1918, was medically graded B2. There is a note in his service record which states; "This man not to be placed in a higher medical grade than B1 owing to being over 40" - this would have effectively kept him in behind the lines support duties. In fact those who served in the front lines were supported by a host of men who were employed behind the lines in work shops, stores depots, field hospitals, training camps, field bakeries, sanitation units and in all the other tasks an army of the time required to maintain its fighting men in the field.

INFANTRY

Typically an infantry soldier would be in the front line trenches for about one quarter of his total time overseas and the number of times he took part in actual combat with the enemy might be limited to a handful of occasions. Despite this, there were other dangers for front line troops, such as sniping, shelling and aerial bombardment, as well as the uncomfortable and basic conditions of trench life to contend with. In a "quiet' sector of the line, boredom could be an issue

ABOVE: Hut life at Crowborough Camp - conditions appear Spartan but the men look content enough

ABOVE: Inside another of the huts at Crowborough Camp - note the low, simply designed wooden bed in the foreground. The man wearing the sling seems happy enough, but his injury reminds us that training could be dangerous. More serious injuries requiring hospitalisation were initially dealt with by the VAD hospital in Crowborough, but soon a military hospital was established in the Camp itself. In most photos and contemporary accounts most men seem to be happy and look well-fed at Crowborough - benefiting from the clean air, regular exercise and decent diet

as well. Infantry units tended to be rotated out of the line every four or five days to give them a respite from the nerve racking and sleep depriving nature of serving at the front.

THE BATTLE OF THE SOMME

The Battle of the Somme is undoubtedly the most iconic battle of World War One. It started on 1st July 1916 and lasted until the 18th November of the same year. The first day of the battle has gone down in history as the bloodiest single day in the existence of the British Army. Nearly 20,000 British soldiers were killed or died of wounds received on that day alone on the Somme front.

Among the fatalities was William Kelly Saunders of Jarvis Brook. Private Saunders died at Gommecourt whilst serving with the London Scottish battalion. Early on the morning of 1st July the men of the battalion had their tot of rum prior to standing to. A smoke screen was put up at 7.25 a.m. Zero hour was 7.30 a.m. when the men went over the top. Despite some initial success they were pushed back to their original positions by midday, having sustained very heavy losses.

A TYPICAL LOCAL FAMILY

My own family provide a pretty average example of a Crowborough family's experience of the war. My great-grandparents, Abraham and Sarah-Ann Adams, were living in a cottage adjacent to the New Mill when the war broke out in 1914.

According to the 1911 Census they had nine of their children in residence with them when the Census was taken - this must have been a tight squeeze, as the cottage (which no longer exists) was, by all accounts, quite small, and some of the "children" were in their late teens and one in his mid 20s.

Five of their sons were to see service

ABOVE: A typical group of ephemera of a Crowborough soldier. The brass tin is a 1914 Princess Mary Christmas tin, issued to all men wearing the King's uniform at Christmas 1914. Many veterans used their tin, which contained tobacco and cigarettes when issued, to store their medals and other mementoes after the war. There are three cap badges above the medals - Cinque Ports, Royal Warwickshire Regiment and Machine Gun Corps - many men were transferred from their original unit to other regiments during the course of the war. To the right of the medals is the "T5 Royal Sussex" brass shoulder title - one of these would have been worn on each shoulder by Crowborough men in the local Territorial Force Battalion. Below this are three brass wound stripes, worn on the lower left sleeve of the service tunic. One was awarded each time a man was wounded, and multiple stripes were not uncommon - the record number awarded to one man during the war is said to be a mind boggling ten! The medals are, British War Medal, Victory Medal, and, from the Second World War, the Defence Medal - many First World War veterans qualified for this by serving in the Home Guard in the Second World War

during the war - Jack, Sid, Nimmy, Oliver and Len - a not unusual number among the large families prevalent at the time. Of the five men, records survive in the National Archives for only two of them - again, this is average, as a large proportion of First World War service records were destroyed in an enemy air raid in the Second World War. So we have quite a detailed picture of the activities of two of them, and the service of the other three has involved a bit of detective work to establish a basic outline of what they did. As happened in many families, talking about the war afterwards was not indulged in very much, most men wanted to put the war behind them, so there is not a great deal of oral history to go by.

The five men reflect the general make-up of the Army during the war - one was a pre-war regular soldier, one joined the TF shortly after the outbreak of war, two others volunteered for service in 1915, and one was conscripted in 1916.

LEFT: William Saunders of Jarvis Brook. He died on the first day of the Battle of the Somme - 1st July 1916. He was among 19000 British soldiers who died that day; another 38000 were listed as missing or wounded

My great uncle Ephraim John Adams (known as Jack) was the first of the brothers to join up. Fortunately his service records survive in the National Archives. He was a groom in civilian life and joined the regular army in 1907, aged 19. His regiment was the Royal West Kents. There is some anecdotal evidence to suggest that this regiment was as popular for Crowborough area men choosing a regular army career as the Royal Sussex Regiment. In those days most regular Army regiments maintained two battalions - one based in the UK, which was generally under strength, and the other garrisoning an outpost of Empire. A recruit would generally spend two years in the home battalion before spending the rest of his service overseas. The overseas battalion therefore contained the majority of a regiment's experienced troops. A good number of the older troops would have seen service in the Boer War or other colonial conflicts at the time of the First World War.

In February 1909 Jack sailed from Southampton for Bombay aboard the SS Plassy to join his regiment's overseas battalion (the 2nd Battalion) in India. Once the war broke out many regiments' overseas regular battalions were replaced by TF units sent out from the UK to free them up so that they could join the fighting in France. However, the 2nd Royal West Kents remained in India until late January 1915, when they were sent to Basra to join the Middle East Expeditionary Force, assembled to fight the Turks. Jack had been seconded to a job at divisional headquarters in October 1910, and was still in that post when the 2nd battalion was posted to the Middle East, so he didn't go with them.

By late 1916 news would have reached him that one of his brothers had been killed in France and another wounded. In January 1917, he requested a reversion to regimental duties - this would have made it more likely that he would have been released to join the

fighting. Instead he was retained in India, promoted to acting sergeant and employed as an instructor at his local brigade bombing school.

Although increasing numbers of regular soldiers in India were released for service in France and elsewhere as the war dragged on, he was fortunate that the Army decided India was the most useful place he could be, as the fighting in the Middle East to which his battalion was committed was every bit as unpleasant as it was on the Western Front. He saw out his Army service in India, finally seeing active service on the North-West Frontier in 1919, for which he was awarded the India General Service Medal. He returned to England in March 1928. His medal index card in the National Archives suggests that he saw some service with the RAF after the war as an aircraftsman.

My grandfather, Nimrod Adams (Nimmy to his friends), was the second Adams brother to join up, on 15th November 1914. Interestingly, his service mirrors that of well-known local golf professional Charles Macey between that date and September 1917, when Charles Macey was selected for officer training, having been chosen for a commission from the ranks.

Charles Macey was the assistant professional at the Beacon Golf club from 1906, and the professional from 1912 - a position he was to hold (with a gap for his war service) until 1941. He also had a son called Charles (Charlie), who was a well-known local character as well as following in his father's footsteps at the golf club. The 1911 Census shows Charles Macey senior living in lodgings at Blackness Road.

Nimmy was a woodland worker on the De La Warr's estate when the war broke out. The fact that both men joined the local TF unit in November 1914 is significant. That month a new battalion of the 5th Royal Sussex Regiment was formed - the 2/5th. It is likely that its formation was accompanied by a big

ABOVE: HM Troopship Plassy, in which Jack Adams sailed for India in 1909 with the Royal West Kents, was launched in November 1900. She was a 450 foot, 6,500 ton steamship able to carry 200 passengers. She operated mostly as a troop transport during the Boer War and then on the Indian Garrison run. During the First World War she was converted for use as a hospital ship and was present at the Battle of Jutland, taking on the wounded from the battle cruisers "Lion" and "Princess Royal"

FACING PAGE: "Old Soldiers never die, they always fade away" from *Tommy's Tunes*, compiled by 2nd Lieutenant F T Nettleingham, Royal Flying Corps, 1917. Old soldier Jack Adams in the 1960s

RIGHT: Charles Macey became assistant pro at the Crowborough Beacon Golf Club at Whitsun 1906 and the pro in 1912. After joining the 2/5th Cinque Ports Battalion, Royal Sussex Regiment, early in the war, he saw service in France with the Royal Warwickshire's before being commissioned as a Second Lieutenant in 1917. He survived the war, and afterwards resumed his role as club professional

recruiting drive, as a number of local men seemed to have joined the unit at that time.

Although neither Charles Macey's or Nimmy's complete records appear to survive in the National Archives, something of their service can be gleaned from what remains, and from other sources, including contemporary mentions of them in *The Courier*.

Both men would most likely have served in a home defence role prior to them going to France in May 1916. They both served in France with the 2/6th Battalion of the Royal Warwickshire Regiment. A history of the 2/6th's role in the war was written in 1929. It refers to final drafts of men being received shortly before embarkation to bring the battalion up to full strength (about 900 men). This included; "a fine lot of men from the Hampshire and Sussex Regiments". It is likely that a number of other Crowborough men were among this draft, in addition to Charles Macey and Nimmy. The battalion proceeded to France on 21st May 1916.

The first major action the battalion took part in was the attack on the German held Wick Salient on 19th July 1916. This was a disastrous diversionary attack, designed to help prevent the Germans from reinforcing the Somme front. The intention to launch this attack had been well-signalled to the Germans in advance, due to various postponements and tardy artillery preparations, and, consequently, they were well prepared. We know from a report in *The Courier* published in November 1916 that Nimmy was wounded on 19th July in this attack (an earlier report in *The Courier* from August 1916 gives his date of wounding as 21st July, but this can't be right as, according to the official Battalion War Diary, the unit was out of the front line resting and bathing on that date - there was often confusion over dates in initial reports of woundings and fatalities - so the 19th July has to be the correct date).

Although the Battalion history carries

LEFT: A dapper looking Oliver Adams photographed just before he volunteered. A motor lorry driver in civilian life, he found a useful role in the Army Service Corps' Motor Transport branch. He felt strongly enough about the violation of Belgian neutrality to name his son, born in 1916, Oliver Belgium Adams

a description of this action, the official Battalion War Diary carries a more detailed account. Every battalion kept an official War Diary during the war. These were written by a junior officer each day. They weren't designed to be emotive They were written in a matter of fact, prosaic style as a factual record of events. This is the Battalion's very poignant account of this action in its War Diary - writing in round brackets is as found in the War Diary; writing in square brackets has been added by way of explanation; it has been kept as written, including the punctuation. The battalion was divided into four companies - A, B, C & D - each about 200 men strong:

Notification received that zero [hour] fixed for 11.00 a.m...at 11.00 a.m. artillery bombardment started...5.31 p.m. The men started to file out through the sally ports [gaps in the breastworks] for the offensive on Wicks Salient and formed four lines in no man's land... immediately the left of the trenches shelled very heavily with the result that in a very short time all the officers had been killed or wounded. The lines advanced across no man's land and when our artillery barrage lifted the leading line was within 80 yards of Wick Salient. Immediately the barrage lifted they were shelled with shrapnel and H E [high explosive] and the enemy formed a barrage across no man's land, at the same time the German trenches became alive with men and a large number of machine guns opened a heavy fire on them mowing down the advancing lines. The support company ('B') followed at 100 yds [yards] distance but was treated in a similar way. Notwithstanding this two platoons [about 60 men] reached the enemy's parapet but owing to the heavy losses caused and the casualties among the officers, the attack was unable to advance. Meanwhile D company in reserve moved two platoons up into the front line...The position was reported to Brigade H.Q. & orders received that the attack would be continued. Telephone communication with the front line now broke down but in spite of the heavy fire was quickly restored. Immediately afterwards orders were received that the attack would be postponed till 8.10 and that survivors would be withdrawn under cover of a barrage by our artillery... at 7.10 the barrage started and all who could returned to the trenches. The attack was now postponed till 9.00 p.m. & later orders were received that the attack would be abandoned.

Some 240 of the Battalion's men were killed, wounded or listed as missing during this action - nearly half of those actually committed to the attack. While they had been waiting to go into no man's land, in a "you couldn't make it up" type incident, battalion headquarters had had to deal with an enquiry from corps headquarters over a

discrepancy in the number of empty pickle jars returned to store by the battalion during the previous month!

The following year, Charles Macey was commissioned from the ranks and he returned to England in September 1917 for officer training. He was posted to the Royal Sussex Regiment as a Second Lieutenant. Nimmy continued to serve with the Royal Warwickshire's until 1918, when he was transferred to an infantry unit of the Machine Gun Corps in the final month's of the War. We know from his obituary in *The Courier* in 1981 that he was wounded three times altogether during his two-an-a-half year stint in France. He was finally demobbed on the 5th March 1919.

Sidney Hugh Adams (Sid) was called up on 7th April 1916, aged 25, and joined the 13th (South Down) Battalion Royal Sussex Regiment. After brief training in the UK he must have been sent out with a draft of replacements to join the

OPPOSITE: Sid Adams photographed at Stickells' studio shortly before he was called up. He was one of many Sussex men, who, with minimal training, were thrown into the Battle of the Somme. He died of wounds received in the autumn of 1916

TOP LEFT: Leonard Adams with his wife. After joining the local Royal Sussex Regiment Territorial Force, he was transferred to the Royal Artillery

TOP RIGHT: Jack Adams in India - a regular soldier, the chevrons on his lower left sleeve are good conduct stripes

LEFT: Nimrod Adams - working as a 17 year old woodman on the Earl De La Warr's estate in 1911. He joined his local Territorial Force unit shortly after the war started, aged 20, and went on to be wounded three times between 1916 and 1918

Battalion in France. According to a report in *The Courier* he was at Purfleet, Essex in August 1916 - Purfleet contained transit camps for men waiting to be sent to Europe via Tilbury Docks.

He was committed to action on the Somme front, along with many other inexperienced troops, where he was fatally wounded. His death certificate states that he died of wounds in France on 1st October 1916. As in a great many cases, news of his death did not reach his wife for some time. According to *The Courier*; "Mrs Adams had not heard from the deceased for over a month, and it was as a result of enquiries made by a local gentleman on her behalf that the melancholy information was obtained from the War Office." Sid's name is on the Crowborough war memorial and also on the St Johns Church memorial plaque.

Oliver Adams' service records survive in the National Archives, although they suffer from burn damage from the Second World War air raid on the building in which the records were kept. His records show that he was a "motor lorry driver" in civilian life. Not surprisingly therefore he joined the Motor Transport Army Service Corps. He enlisted at Grove Park, their London headquarters, at the end of March 1915.

He embarked for France from Avonmouth in August 1915, and between then and his demobilisation he served with a variety of units, including a Field Ambulance Company, A Royal Artillery unit (presumably transporting the ammunition) and 3rd Corps Headquarters where it is likely he drove a staff car. He was demobilised in July 1919. His records show that he had a minor run-in with the military authorities and was fined three days pay for failing to tighten a part on a government vehicle - we don't know what this part was, because the relevant page is incomplete and suffers from burn damage.

Leonard Adams (Len) is the brother who's service we know least about. We have an undated photo of him in uniform wearing

a Royal Sussex Regiment cap badge - from what little we can see of his brass shoulder titles he would appear to be a TF soldier. There are two mentions of him in *The Courier*, the first, in August 1916, refers to him being in the Royal Garrison Artillery and based in Norfolk, so quite likely that he was in a coastal defence battery at that time. The second mention in the paper, in November 1916, refers to him as being in the Royal Field Artillery and based at High Wycombe - this was the home of the TF Royal Field Artillery's No 4 Brigade. We know from his campaign medal entitlement

in the National Archives (his medal index card) that he saw service overseas at some point, but that is all we know.

THE VAD HOSPITAL

The VAD (Voluntary Aid Detachment) was a relatively new national organisation when the war broke out. It had been set up in 1909 to provide for a rapid expansion of military nursing capacity in time of war, in much the same way that the Territorial Force (precursors of today's Territorial Army) had been set-up in 1908 to allow a rapid expansion of the army. Like the Territorial Force it was a voluntary organisation which would be mobilised in time of war, and whose members trained in their spare time.

Sussex 46 detachment (which covered Crowborough) was mobilised at the end of 1914. In November 1914, rumours swirled around the town that Walsh Manor was to be fitted up as a hospital and that wounded soldiers would shortly be received there. In fact it wasn't until February 1915 that Walsh Manor VAD was up and running under its Commandant Miss Laver. On February 12th *The Courier* newspaper

ABOVE: Walsh Manor VAD Hospital - some men in their 'hospital blues' are on the terrace

ABOVE: A comic postcard showing a wounded soldier in "hospital blues" - a special uniform for hospitalised soldiers, it helped maintain a sense of military discipline among recuperating troops, especially in the auxiliary hospitals which were smaller and had a more relaxed atmosphere. It also enabled wounded troops well enough to be out and about to be easily recognised by the public as men who had done their bit

reported; "Crowborough VAD Hospital at Walsh Manor is being occupied this week. Several patients are being admitted from the hutments at Brown Knoll (Crowborough Warren)." It was able to accommodate 20 patients, later increased to 23. It received sick and wounded soldiers from Crowborough Camp.

ACCIDENTS

The wounded were presumably as a result of training accidents at the Camp - it is known that injuries during training were not uncommon, and included mishaps when practising with live grenades. Staff at this time consisted of a Matron, two trained nurses, one housemaid and two cooks, who were all resident at the hospital. Over 170 patients were treated in its first year of operation. The hospital was en route from the Camp to the railway station and it would have been handy for the Royal Army Medical Corps or Army Service Corps to drop off or pick up patients on their way to or from the Army Service Corps depot near the station where many supplies and munitions for the camp would have arrived by train.

However, we know that by the summer

of 1915, the army had its own field hospital at the Camp under the command of Lt Fox, Royal Army Medical Corps. Sometimes civilians were admitted to the Camp hospital - in August 1915, for instance, *The Courier* reported that a man staying in Crowborough, who had been shot on a civilian shooting range, was admitted. By early 1917, the Camp hospital was commanded by Captain Charles Franklin Magee - the fact that it was now commanded by a Captain rather than a Lieutenant suggests that, over the previous 18 months, it had become a larger establishment with more personnel.

ABOVE: Staff and patients at Walsh VAD in relaxed mode - most of the men are wearing their special hospital uniforms of blue jackets and red ties. The two men in normal uniform are probably visiting their comrades. Patients at this time were taken from Crowborough Camp. The body language of the nurses is interesting. The three amateur VAD nurses stand together, while the clipped and professional looking nurse to the right of them is probably one of the two British Red Cross Society trained nurses on the staff. At the start of the war many professional nurses looked down on the minimally trained VAD nurses, but the "VADs", as they were known, gradually gained their respect through their hard work and sacrifice as the war progressed. Cap badges are a good way of identifying a soldier's regiment - of the three caps on the ground in this photo two badges are identifiable with a magnifying glass, one is the Royal Sussex Regiment, the other the Buffs (East Kent Regiment)

HARECOMBE MANOR

Walsh Manor VAD was closed in December 1916 - although it continued to be used as a venue for nursing training courses well into 1917. Following its closure the War Office asked the 46 Detachment to find a new "more commodious residence". In the latter half of May 1917 the VAD hospital moved to Harecombe Manor in Southview Road. The move was accompanied by a "View Day" at the new hospital, and, according to *The Courier*; "a considerable number of residents and visitors took the opportunity of inspecting the institution". A squad of the Crowborough men's VAD (Sussex 17) was on duty in the grounds and there was a concert by the band of the Canadian Engineers, who played a "delightful programme of music" to raise funds for the hospital. As well as a new location, the hospital had changed in character - it now provided 40 beds for other ranks.

In August 1917, *The Courier* reported on its first three months of operation. In those three months 108 patients had been admitted from the Kitchener Military Hospital in Brighton (69 British; 32 Australian and 7 Canadian). Of these 9 were men convalescing from illness and 99 had been wounded or accidentally injured.

Up until 1916 the Kitchener Hospital had accommodated wounded Indian soldiers of the British Indian Army - however it was decided that Indian troops should be

TOP: Harecombe Manor VAD Hospital in Southview Road

ABOVE: Another view of Harecombe Manor VAD with its attractive gardens evident

LEFT: Private Len Marriner - the badge he is wearing on his lapel is the Silver War Badge - struck in Sterling silver, it was issued to troops honourably discharged due to wounds or sickness. Each badge was individually numbered on the reverse - it was a serious offence to wear a badge you were not entitled to, as it was intended to show that a man of military age had "done his bit" and was in civvies for a good reason. Private Marriner was wounded in the Balkans campaign whilst serving with the Hampshire Regiment, and had been found civilian employment at Crowborough Camp in the canteen lines. The photo was taken by Stickells in 1918

ABOVE: New Mill, Crowborough Warren. This postcard, sent in August 1915 by a Miss Goulston, says; "Crowborough is such a pretty place... yesterday we drove to see a most beautiful garden where there was a very good soldiers' band playing in aid of the refugees." She is presumably referring to a concert in aid of Belgian refugees

RIGHT: The New Mill at Crowborough Warren from a different angle

employed fighting the Turks in the Middle East, and so most Indian troops, apart from some cavalry units, were withdrawn from the Western Front, negating the need for the Indian Hospital in Brighton. In September 1917 The Kitchener Hospital became the 10th Canadian General Hospital.

REFUGEES

The Belgian refugee phenomenon of the First World War is very little known about or remembered today. During 1914 -18 however, it was a major issue that everyone in Britain would have been aware of.

When the German army swept through neutral Belgium in August 1914, their actions created a wave of civilian refugees desperate to flee the advancing German forces. The dreaded Uhlan cavalry were often first to arrive in a Belgian village or town, followed by waves of German infantry. Fearing ambush by civilians, the Germans raided houses and farms. In some instances they looted and burned homes, killed inhabitants or took them hostage as human shields. Many fleeing Belgian civilians headed to the coast, hoping to embark for England. There was a huge tide of public sympathy for the Belgian people in Britain. In September 1914 the British Government offered; "Victims of war the hospitality of the British nation."

The Local Government Board and the Great Eastern Railway agreed to provide a service of steamers and trains for the transport of refugees, and this was from Antwerp to Tilbury and then onwards to Victoria by train - following the fall of Antwerp, Ostend was used instead.

From Victoria, the Belgians were sent to a clearing house in London before being dispersed around the country, or 'distributed' in the official parlance of the day. In addition to the refugees thousands of wounded Belgian soldiers were evacuated to the UK for treatment and convalescence.

ABOVE: Belgian refugees flee the advancing German Army in 1914. Some 250,000 refugees were accepted by the UK during the war and a number of Belgian families were housed at Crowborough

The refugees were sent as far afield as Ireland, for instance, the workhouse at Dunshaughlin in County Meath was fitted out to house up to 125 refugees. Indeed it seems that there weren't many parts of the British isles, however distant and remote, that didn't offer accommodation the the Belgian exiles. Some sources estimate the refugee exodus from Belgium amounted to a quarter of a million people. Local committees were set-up to find accommodation and provide financial and other help for the refugee families.

Crowborough is known to have done its bit for the Belgian refugees. In March 1915 the parish council expressed its appreciation to householders; "who had allowed their houses to be occupied by Belgian refugees". There is also reference in the council minute books in August 1917 to a Belgian family occupying Holly Lodge, Station Road, Jarvis Brook. It is also known that Lady Conan Doyle helped organise a home for Belgian refugees at Hurtis Hill, near to the Conan Doyle's own home at Windlesham.

Fund raising was undertaken for the refugees in the town, and a visitor to Crowborough refers to a band concert in aid of them in 1915 in a postcard

LEFT: A squad of the Buffs (East Kent Regiment) pose outside their hut at Crowborough Camp in May 1916. Two of the men in the back row are wearing spectacles. Although some spectacle wearers served from 1914 as front line infantrymen, it wasn't as acceptable or commonplace in the British Army as in some other armies. However, the number of bespectacled men increased as the war wore on, due to the pressing need for manpower. In combat, most spectacle wearers would carry at least one spare pair of glasses with them

home. We know from reports in the local newspaper that various concerts, lectures and other fund-raising activities were undertaken. On 26th February 1915, *The Courier* reported that; "A delightful concert was given at the Parker Lecture Hall by the Royal Army Medical Corps" in aid of the National Belgian Relief Fund and a sum of £10 and ten shillings was raised. St Johns School also got involved in the fund-raising - in July 1916 a concert was performed by the children in the vicarage grounds in aid of the Belgian Children's Relief Fund.

Ordinary people were very taken with the plight of Belgium, and it was considered patriotic to sympathise with Belgium's plight. "Belgium" as a given name for babies became quite popular - my great uncle, Oliver Adams, had a son in 1916 whom he named Oliver Belgium Adams. As the war progressed the Belgian refugee crisis became overshadowed by the fighting on the Western Front, with nearly every family being affected by the ever growing casualty lists. When the war ended the vast majority of the refugees in Britain seem to have quickly returned to their homeland where they faced the task of re-building their shattered lives.

ABOVE: War Savings were a key part of funding Britain's war effort. Crowborough raised a phenomenal amount of money in relation to the size of its population

'COMFORTS FOR THE TROOPS'

A great many local people were involved, one way or another, in providing morale boosting treats for the troops. *The Courier* reported in 1918 for instance that; "Miss M. E. Stuart has rendered the local soldiers on active service such signal service with the supply of tobacco and cigarettes". Apparently, Miss Stuart raised enough funds to send out 131,000 cigarettes and 193 lbs of tobacco during 1916 and 1917.

As well as this, a great deal of fund raising was done to support the war itself. Crowborough's local War Savings Committee was tireless in this respect - in 1918 for instance, it set itself a target of raising £10,000 - the cost of two tanks, which it duly managed to achieve - a great deal of money given the size of the local population at the time and a few hundred thousand pounds in today's values.

The First World War on the home front was characterised by what today would be called the Big Society. Government was not seen as the provider of all things, and, a great many services and funds for war-related activities were organised or had funds raised for them by the effort of local committees and energetic individuals.

Things that you would assume the government would cover the cost of, such as the VAD hospital, derived a good deal of their funds from the goodwill of the public. For instance, the VAD hospital at Harecombe had 60 beds occupied by June 1918. At that time, the Commandant, Lady Gatacre, appealed for gifts of vegetables to help feed the wounded patients.

In 1918, two German helmets, "one camouflaged" were received by parcel post at the VAD hospital from a Field Post Office in France. They contained a slip of paper requesting they be sold in aid of the hospital. The note was signed "A Crowborough Lad".

Local civilian volunteers also helped out at the two YMCA huts at Crowborough Camp and in the town.

BELOW: A comic take on army life at Crowborough Camp

ABOVE: "The hutments" at Crowborough Camp

LIFE AT THE CAMP

Fortunately a good many letters and other accounts have survived which paint a picture of life at the Warren Camp. In particular, the Imperial War Museum has an extensive audio recording of an interview with a soldier, Joe Fitzpatrick, who was based there during the height of the war. Joe was a member of the 2/6th Battalion of the Manchester Regiment. His battalion was posted to Crowborough Camp in the summer of 1915, and remained there for about 10 months. His account is interesting in that it paints a picture of the ordinary life of a soldier at the Camp.

Breakfast consisted of porridge or bacon and eggs. Teatime was often spent in the Camp's Young Men's Christian Association (YMCA) hut where the men could buy a cup of tea and a jam sandwich or a bun, cigarettes, and postcards and note paper. Dinner was a cooked meal such as Yorkshire pudding, potatoes and beef - unless they were on a 10-15 mile route march, in which case rations might be eaten during a break from marching.

Initially personal kit consisted of Japanese rifles and leather equipment, reflecting a shortage of home produced equipment at this stage of the war. Eventually these were replaced with British webbing which was better designed and more comfortable. Lee Enfield rifles would replace the Japanese ones, much to the relief of the men. A member of another battalion issued with the Japanese rifles commented; "Japanese rifles were served out, but their intricate mechanism proved a source of much trouble to all concerned."

Men were accommodated two platoons to a hut (about 60-70 men). Beds consisted of three wooden boards between two low wooden trestles. Each man had a straw filled mattress and pillow. Each man was allotted a certain day and time of the week for a shower. Like most men posted

ABOVE: Nice photo showing a group of soldiers about to set off in a taxi from Crowborough Camp - maybe to enjoy a theatre show in Tunbridge Wells, or to visit a country pub. The soldier partly visible in the background on the extreme left of the photo is wearing "hospital blues", suggesting he has only just been returned to the camp from hospital or has been allowed out of the Camp hospital for a recuperative stroll. Training with bayonets and grenades and musketry drill resulted in occasional casualties, including some fatalities

RIGHT: An al fresco celebration between the hut lines at Crowborough Camp. On the Imperial War Museum website there is an audio recording of one soldier's experiences at Crowbrough Camp which is well worth a listen if you get the chance (www.iwm.org.uk/collections/item/object/80010544)

ABOVE: A group of men working under the supervision of a sergeant attempt to rectify the muddy conditions. The sergeant writes on the back of the photo; "Self with fatigue party clearing away mud and laying cinder paths in camp. I often get a gang like this to superintend. We have been for a night march...a lot of our men fell into a brook up to their middle, and then we all got into a big bog over our boot tops. It was pitch dark and we marched by compass over scrubby country."

LEFT: A group of Royal Army Medical Corps orderlies outside their hut - these men probably manned the Camp's own hospital

ABOVE AND RIGHT: As a country we are noted for our sense of humour even in the face of great hardship or adversity. Comic postcards were a feature of the First World War and played a major part in maintaining the morale of troops and civilians alike. Thousands of designs were produced during the conflict and millions of copies posted. These two cards were personalised by the publisher to be relevant to soldiers based at Crowborough Camp

RIGHT: More sentimental postcards, like this studio posed scene, were also produced in huge numbers. Postcards like this one were an economical way for soldiers to keep in touch with their loved ones, and quicker to write than a letter. The cards themselves would have cost a halfpenny or penny each, and another halfpenny for a stamp. To modern eyes First World War postcard subjects may seem naïve, over sentimental and sometimes even distasteful. However, they were sent in quantities not seen in any war before or since, and as such have left us with an important physical link to the ordinary people who lived through those times

LEFT: Another type of card popular with the troops was one showing their regiment's name and badge - this card, sent by Private Daniel Ray Jordan is typical of the genre. Private Jordan was with the 4/4th Battalion of The Queen's Royal West Surrey Regiment based at Crowborough Camp in early 1916, and from where he sent this card to his eight year old daughter. Daniel Jordan was a postman from Eastbourne before the War. After training at Crowborough he was sent in a draft of men to France to join his regiment's 1st Battalion. He was killed in action with them on 25th September 1917

OPPOSITE: Private Royle with his sweetheart, Miss Smith, photographed when he was home on leave in 1918. Private Royle,from Eccles, is thought to have joined the Manchester Regiment in late 1914. In May 1915 his battalion moved to Crowborough, and he was sent to France in August 1915. He was later transferred to the Lancashire Fusiliers

LEFT: Private Royle's headstone. Sadly, he was killed on 11 September 1918 during a bombing raid while scouting in the German lines at Blauport Farm

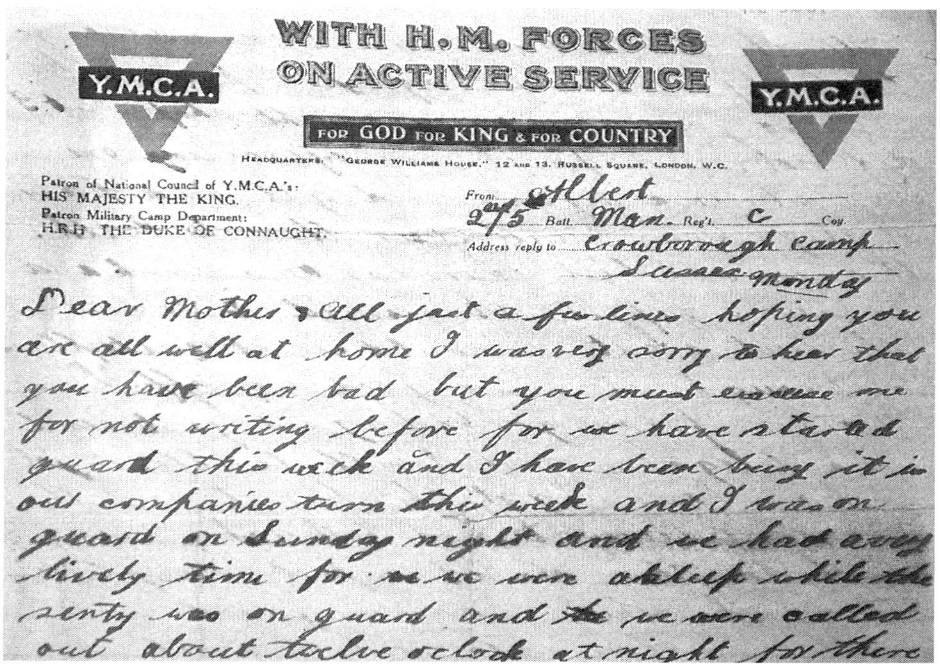

WITH H.M. FORCES ON ACTIVE SERVICE

Y.M.C.A. Y.M.C.A.

FOR GOD FOR KING & FOR COUNTRY

HEADQUARTERS: "GEORGE WILLIAMS HOUSE," 12 AND 13, RUSSELL SQUARE, LONDON, W.C.

Patron of National Council of Y.M.C.A.'s:
HIS MAJESTY THE KING.
Patron Military Camp Department:
H.R.H. THE DUKE OF CONNAUGHT.

From Albert
2/5 Batt. Man. Reg't. C Coy.
Address reply to Crowborough Camp
Sussex Monday

Dear Mother & all just a few lines hoping you are all well at home I was very sorry to hear that you have been bad but you must excuse me for not writing before for we have started guard this week and I have been being it in our companies turn this week and I was on guard on Sunday night and we had a very lively time for we we were asleep while the sentry was on guard and we were called out about twelve oclock at night for there

LEFT: Letter on YMCA headed paper written by Private Albert Royle from Crowborough Camp in 1915. In his letter he recounts an exciting incident at the Camp; "...we have started guard duties this week (it being) our companies turn... I was on guard on Sunday night and we had a very lively time... we were called out about twelve o'clock at night for there were four spies in the Camp... they were down at the stables at the other end of the Camp and they held the stable guard up with revolvers, but he whistled for the other guards and they hopped it quick... we were after them all night." He also recounts the distant sighting of a Zeppelin; "We were out last Thursday on a march and we saw a zeppelin... we could see it quite plain although it was a good way off."

to Crowborough Camp, Joe Fitzpatrick mentions the muddy conditions; he also mentions the aloofness from the men of the officers, which was a standard feature of British Army life at the time.

Training revolved around creating an efficient fighting force which would be steady under fire. For the most part this consisted of PT before breakfast, long route marches in full equipment, rifle practice (or musketry as it was still called in official parlance), bayonet practice, grenade throwing and familiarisation with trench warfare (practice trenches were dug at Kings Standing and elsewhere). Later in the war familiarisation with gas masks and practice gas attack drills were incorporated into the men's training.

The main purpose of Crowborough Camp, and many others like it that sprang up all over the country, was to manage the transition from civilian to soldier. Men from the camps would be sent in drafts to the channel ports for embarkation overseas once they had finished their training. Once in a war theatre infantry men would receive further acclimatisation training in the rear areas behind the front lines before being committed to actual combat operations.

Joe Fitzpatrick says in his interview that he found the local Crowborough people were

LEFT: A group of 3/1st Sussex Yeomanry troopers at Crowborough Camp in 1916. The yeomanry were the cavalry arm of the Territorial Force - though most yeomanry units fought as infantry for most of the war. The 3/1st supplied trained drafts of men to the 1/1st which was on active service in the Middle East at this time. Officers of the 1/1st complained that many of their drafts were diverted for service in France & Flanders. This group at least seems to be going to its first line unit in Egypt judging by the pith helmets some of the men are wearing. The high jinks being displayed in the photo by some of the men suggests they are celebrating something, maybe the completion of their basic training

very friendly and respectful to the soldiers based in the local area.

UNSUNG HEROES

The Army was full of unsung heroes during the war, and many of these belonged to the Army Service Corps (ASC). The ASC was the backbone of the Army, transporting supplies, ammunition and food. Crowborough had a contingent of ASC men, based at the Camp and at their depot near the station at Jarvis Brook. One such ASC man was Charles Gent, an ASC Driver.

Driver Gent's service records survive in the National Archive – like many of the surviving records they obviously suffered water damage which means some of the writing has faded away. Driver Gent hailed from Greenwich and had joined the TF in December 1914. TF soldiers could sign the Imperial Service obligation agreeing to serve outside the UK in time of war. Although he signed the form, he didn't go abroad until 1917 - probably due to his medical category being quite low.

Often troops would arrive at the station at Jarvis Brook on special trains in battalion strength units (800-900 men) and march with their personal gear to the camp. As Charles Gent was a Driver - this meant

he either rode horses on a team pulling wagons or sat on a wagon driving the horse pulling it – he might have been involved in moving their heavier equipment to the camp and back again when the time came for them to depart. He would probably also have been involved in moving the vast amount of ordnance that the camp required, especially after the Machine Gun School had been set-up there.

The route from the station to the Camp is believed to have been Walshes Road, Fermor Road, Hurtis Hill, Sheep Plain (Sir Arthur Conan Doyle lived at Sheep Plain, and he would have had to have driven past his house to and from the Camp). The Army asked for Hurtis Hill to be widened during the war years, which lends weight to this being the route generally taken.

Charles Gent survived his period in France and was demobbed in June 1919.

TRAGEDIES

The mill pond had a tragic history of drowning incidents before the war. There is some evidence to suggest that it was put out of bounds by commanding officers of some units passing through the Camp. Despite this, during the war it remained a magnet for off duty troops, and, sadly, a number of fatalities occurred due to men drowning there. For example in August 1916, the local paper related the sad case of Private Ernest King of the Buffs (the East Kent Regiment); "With several of his comrades Private King was bathing in the New Mill pond...he had been in the water for some 20 minutes when he remarked to two of his friends, who were on a raft, that he was going back to the shore. He had got a short distance from the raft when he was seen to be in difficulty. His companions called for assistance, but before anyone could reach him he went down. A Private in the East Kent Yeomanry jumped in...but failed to find the unfortunate soldier."

ABOVE: Warren Road - the sender of this postcard, a Territorial Force soldier and keen swimmer on pre-war summer camp, highlights the dangers of swimming in the mill ponds; "There has been so many drowned (in the past) that bathing is forbidden to us just my luck."

OPPOSITE: Driver Charles Gent outside his hut at Crowborough Camp, wearing a 1903 pattern bandolier - this was worn by all Army Service Corps, Royal Field Artillery and Royal Engineers Drivers during the war. The ASC depot at Jarvis Brook handled supplies for the Camp and also included a field bakery to supply the men with their daily bread

The body was recovered a few hours later and removed to New Mill Cottage, where an inquest was held by the Deputy Coroner for East Sussex two days later. The deceased was only 17 years old.

In June 1917, Sapper Robert Watson, aged 19, of the Canadian Engineers, drowned at the New Mill pond - this was said to have been the fourth case of its kind since the war started. Following this event, the lake was put out of bounds to all troops based in the area. Sadly, our Canadian allies also suffered other accidental casualties. A 41 year old from the Canadian Machine Gun Depot, Private Lee Smith, was killed while walking in February 1917, suffering a fractured skull having been hit by a motorcycle.

AIR RAIDS

In February 1915, the German Kaiser told his commanders; "The air war against England will be carried out with the greatest energy."

By May 1915, the German High Command had made the strategic decision to bomb the British mainland using airships. The initial target list included: military bases; fuel, ammunition and other military stores, military barracks; and the London Docklands. In fact the airships weren't all that particular where they dropped their bombs and most casualties were civilian. Although the casualties from this campaign were comparatively light compared to those inflicted by the Blitz in the Second World War, they none the less had a great impact at the time. In London a blackout was imposed, and many Londoners sought refuge in the underground railway system - a portent of things to come in the Second World war.

Although I can't find any record of Crowborough being bombed, in May 1915 the military authorities wrote to Crowborough's parish council suggesting

ABOVE: Despite its placid appearance, the mill pond claimed a number of soldiers' lives during the war

RIGHT: Second Lieutenant John Bone poses for the photographer with his motorbike at Crowborough Camp in spring 1916 - motorbikes were popular with young officers. John Bone was the son of a Wesleyan minister and was born in China. Before the war he worked for Jardine Matheson in Hong Kong. On the outbreak of hostilities he returned home and joined the 3/6th East Surrey Regiment. His unit moved to Crowborough in April 1916. On 10th July 1916 he was sent to France on attachment to the Notts & Derby Regiment, who had recently suffered massive casualties. John Bone was killed in action on 22nd July, less than two weeks after arriving at the front

CE-4111

LEFT: Off duty soldiers, probably from the Buffs (East Kent Regiment), fraternising with local girls at the mill pond

COMPANY. LIMITED.
SOUTHON.
CONFECTIONER

LEFT: New Mill pond was a local beauty spot and a magnet for off-duty soldiers who liked to swim there. The sender of this card, an Army Service Corps Driver serving with the 66th East Lancashire Division, writes; "This is a picture of the pond where we go swimming, the week before I was at home (on leave)...a soldier was drowned and they only found him the Sunday after I got back." He could be referring to 18 year old Daniel Riley, a private in D Company 2/6th Lancashire Fusiliers who would have been in the same division as the writer. It is known from coroner's reports that a number of soldiers drowned at the mill pond during the course of the war

BELOW: In this wartime poster the fear of air raids is turned into an appeal for recruits

LEFT: Crowborough's Volunteer Fire Brigade outside Southon's at Crowborough Cross. The Brigade was given responsibility for air raid precautions and organising salvage parties in the event of Zeppelin raids on the town. Two of the men in the front row wear their fire brigade long service medals proudly

that they might be asked to arrange fire and salvage parties; "ready to act in case of air raids". The parish council in turn wrote to the Captain of the volunteer fire brigade, local solicitor Frank Humphry, who acknowledged saying that; "The matter of air raids would receive his attention."

By November 1915, the parish council was sufficiently concerned that it resolved to insure the caretaker's cottage and pavilion at Wolfe recreation ground "against damage by aircraft". Meanwhile, Standing Orders at Crowborough Camp simply instructed the men based there to; "Hide in the wood in the event of an air raid."

ABOVE: A Canadian machine gunner's cap badge - thousands of Canadian soldiers passed through Crowborough Camp for training as machine gunners and engineers during the war years

CANADIANS ARRIVE

Canadian soldiers started arriving at Crowborough Camp in late 1916. *The Courier* newspaper reported in November that the Crowborough branch of the

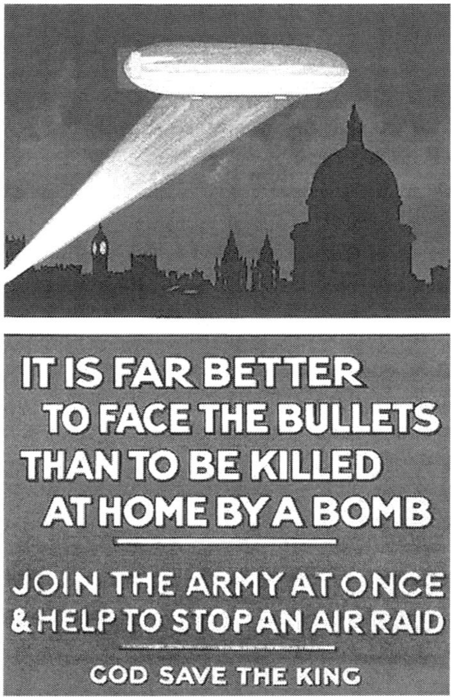

ABOVE: *Machine Gunners' Pocket Book* - thousands of trainee Canadian machine gunners passed through Crowborough Camp between 1916-1918

RIGHT: Looking towards the town centre from Station Road

Victoria League, under its chairman the Rev S F Akroyd, had organised a reception to welcome them to the district at the YMCA Waterloo hut at Crowborough Cross.

The scale of the Canadian presence can be gauged by the fact that some 300 officers accepted the invitation. Sir Arthur and Lady Conan Doyle were also present. The Victoria League had been established some years previously to promote closer union between the different parts of the British Empire, and to foster; "hospitality, understanding and good fellowship" between them.

There were two main elements to the Canadian presence at Crowborough - a machine gun training school, and an engineer's training depot - the latter ran courses on mining and tunnelling.

This letter from Lance Corporal Cephas Finnemore of the Canadian Machine Gun Depot at Crowborough, written in early January 1917, represents a typical Canadian soldier's experience of their life during their time at Crowborough Camp.

Dear Sister:
I am in the Y.M.C.A. [hut] with nothing to do until bedtime so I may as well be doing some writing. I have had an awful time trying to get my writing done. It gets dark so early here that you might as well call it all night, and it certainly can get dark here. I had to get a flashlight to keep from running into people in the dark. The roads are very narrow and all up or down hill. I was up to London last week and it is very nearly as bad up there the lights are cut down so dim and all store lights covered. It certainly is a large city. I travelled all day and then did not see very much of it. I had a ride on the underground railway. That is the only place where it is light and dry. It is a double track electric road; and the cars certainly can travel. They are only about three minutes apart, and you can go to nearly any place underground (in London). It is an awful place for women drinking. You could see them coming out of the bars all over the place carrying their little jug or bottle. I would like to have a week up there to see it all.

We are in a quiet place here, four miles from

the station, and two miles from a small village [Crowborough]. We have a very nice Y.M.C.A here. They hold church in it on Sundays. Well, the holidays are over again for a while, but they did not affect me very much. We had a holiday Christmas Day and a big dinner and that is all I can say for it. I was expected to get some leave, but they stopped all leave after the first two bunches went away. I was to go on the third lot, but no such luck. So I stayed here in camp and made the best of it. We had to attend drill just the same New Year's Day and to make it worse I was having my examinations on the machine gun. But I guess I got through all right. I am taking an N.C.O. (non-commissioned officer) course and it is pretty hard for me. We get lectures every day and have to recopy the notes and study them at night. It generally is a two hours job and I feel like going to bed after I get through. I do not expect I will pass in all subjects, but as long as I get through on the gun all right, I do not care as I will be qualified to go to France then. I have no idea when I will be going over, but I do not expect that it will be for a month or six weeks.

We are having rather bad weather here raining every day. The mud is fierce. I have not received the box you spoke of yet. They are very slow in handling parcels. There is big talk of German peace these days, but I think it will be the Allies' peace in the spring for there is certainly going to be something doing, as soon as it dries up again. I am feeling fine now and getting fat. I guess it must be that Christmas dinner that did it. How are all the folks? Well I guess I will have to ring off for this time.
Cephas.

ABOVE: Crowborough has a long affiliation with the Canadian Army, spanning both World Wars. This Christmas card was produced for members of the Canadian Machine Gun School at Crowborough Camp. This was a large establishment, supplying drafts of trained machine gunners to the Machine Gun Pool at Camiers in France. There was also a Canadian Engineers Training Depot at Crowborough Camp during the First World War

ABOVE: The High Street - this card was sent by a soldier to his daughter in 1917 - he comments; "The picture will give you some idea of what the village looks like. There is only one street and last night it was crowded with soldiers." By the spring of 1917 food shortages were becoming more noticeable, and in April 1917 a Canadian machine-gunner based at Crowborough Camp wrote home; "We used to get half a loaf of bread a day (each), but now it is five men for two loaves... after harvest I guess it will be better."

We know from other letters sent that the Canadians regarded our winter weather as not really winter at all compared to their winters back in Canada. One soldier, William McLellan, wrote home in January 1917; "They say it's the coldest its been in England for 26 years and its only a few degrees below freezing. I've seen lots of colder days up north (in Canada) in July."

RATIONING

Food and other shortages began to manifest themselves as the war went on, especially after the Germans launched their unrestricted U Boat campaign against merchant shipping bringing supplies to the UK from North America. Crowborough was relatively well placed as far as what today would be called "food security". It was an area of market gardens and small mixed farms producing a wide range of crops and livestock. In addition ordinary Crowborough people were essentially still country people, many grew their own fruit and vegetables, or kept hens and other livestock.

In June 1917, the Army Council instructed troops billeted in "houses with large gardens" to grow vegetables for the war effort. Crowborough was mainly affected by coal supply shortages. In September 1917 the

parish minutes record that the parish council was; “anxious to do what they can to secure a supply of coal for the working classes in the parish”, as there had been difficulties at times the previous winter.

The Government instituted compulsory rationing relatively late in the war in 1918 (in World War Two rationing was introduced early on in 1940). After February 1918, it became impossible in London and parts of the south-east to buy butter, margarine, or meat without ration cards; by the end of April, people were required to register for bacon as well, but it was the coal issue that seems to have affected Crowborough people the most.

ABOVE: Many of Crowborough's roads were narrower than today, as this photo taken at Friars Gate shows. These previously lightly used roads suffered particular damage from the large traction engines used by the Army's civilian contractors, such as the Army Timber Agent, to move heavy materials about. The traction engines were also blamed by the Ashdown Forest Conservators for starting forest fires due to sparks from their engines

ROADS

The state of Crowborough's roads during the war years was the subject of many complaints at the time. The roads then weren't asphalted, they were formed from small angular stones, compacted to form a road surface. Almost immediately the war started the volume of complaints about them climbed rapidly. Owing to the burden of military traffic a huge amount of wear and tear was caused. In March 1915, *The Courier* newspaper described the local roads as being; “Famed far and wide for their bad condition” and stated that they had been; “badly cut up by the heavy (military) traffic.”

In May 1915, Sir Arthur Conan Doyle complained to the local authorities about the state of the road in front of his house, Windlesham, on Hurtis Hill. This road must have seen a considerable amount of military traffic, as it is was likely used for the Army Service Corps lorries and wagons to go between the Camp and the army depot at the train station. Massive amounts of food and equipment were needed by the troops at the camp, who numbered several thousand at any one time. After the Canadians arrival and the setting up of the Canadian Machine Gun School at the camp, huge additional supplies of ordnance would have been required as well for practice firing of machine guns.

Contemporary accounts mention the widespread use of traction vehicles during the war, and obviously these heavy machines,

which were essential for moving heavier military supplies, would have had an impact on the roads and contributed to their poor condition.

In 1914, Sir Arthur had apparently had the road outside his house repaired at his own expense, but by Spring 1915 this stone had "utterly disappeared", and "now, if it is not a sea of mud it is a cloud of dust, which penetrates the house (Windlesham) in every part."

TOURISM

It is clear from contemporary reports, as well as from postcards sent by visitors during the war years, that some sort of tourist industry continued throughout the war. In December 1917, for instance, *The Courier* reported that; "The visitors to Crowborough were not as numerous as last year, but the Crest Hotel was fully booked, and at the Beacon Hotel many relatives and friends of officers quartered at Crowborough Camp spent an enjoyable time."

PERSONALITIES

Sir Arthur Conan Doyle had moved to Crowborough in 1906, and, at the time of the First World War, was firmly established as Crowborough's most famous resident. Too old for active service, he threw himself into various other war related activities both locally and nationally. Famously, he served in Crowborough's First World War equivalent of the Home Guard - the Volunteer Training Corps - as a private. He was a tireless writer, lecturer and fundraiser on war related and refugee issues. He is also said to have sent secret messages to British prisoners of war in Germany - he would send them copies of his books with a series of pin pricks through certain letters in the text. These would spell out war news and stories of interest from home.

Rev Akroyd - the Reverend Samuel Fisher Akroyd was the incumbent of All Saints Church at the time of the First World War. He became something of a 'soldier's friend', and he is known to have corresponded

TOP: Crowborough Hill (or Station Road as it was then known) looking towards Rotherfield

ABOVE: A piece of goss crested China in the image of a tank and bearing a Crowborough crest. These small white porcelain models bore the crest of the place they were sold as souvenirs. Very popular during the Edwardian era, during the war a number of military subjects were manufactured. It is said that in 1910, some 95% of homes had at least one piece of crested china on their mantelpiece or sideboard

LEFT: The Rev Samuel Fisher Akroyd was the Vicar of All Saints from 1887 until his death in March 1926 aged 81

ABOVE: A letter to the Rev Samuel Fisher Akroyd - Vicar of All Saints. The Rev Akroyd was something of a Soldiers' Friend during the war years, conducting correspondence with numerous ordinary soldiers. He seems to have been held in very high esteem by the men who knew him. He was instrumental in providing the Church land for the war memorial after the war

ABOVE: Arthur Conan Doyle worked tirelessly for war related causes, as well as serving in Crowborough's World War One equivalent of the Home Guard as a private for the entire war

with numerous ordinary soldiers - British and Canadian. He was instrumental in providing the site for the War Memorial after the war, when, in April 1920, he offered the local war memorial committee the present site at Chapel Green.

Frank Humphry was a well-known local solicitor and Captain of the Town's volunteer fire brigade at the time of the First World War. As a solicitor he represented several soldiers up before the magistrates for, mostly, minor misdemeanours. He and his men would have been responsible for fire fighting and salvage parties had there been Zeppelin air raids on the town.

Allen Hardwicke - After qualifying as a solicitor in December 1903, Hardwicke, who hailed from Sheffield, moved to Crowborough. At the outbreak of the First World War he became the honorary recruiting officer for Crowborough.

Jack Lambert - was born in Queens Road in 1898. He grew up to be only 2ft 10in tall when he was fully grown. He became a well known Crowborough visitor attraction in his own right. Local tailors, the Bradley brothers, made him some smart outfits, including military ones. By 1917 each week *The Courier* newspaper printed an absentee list of men called up who were thought not to have reported to the recruiting office.

In March 1917, some wag thought it would be a good idea if 2ft 10in high Jack Lambert were to report to the recruiting office at

Eastbourne as an absentee. Accordingly, a very tall Canadian soldier agreed to escort him to Eastbourne. *The Courier* reported; "Dressed in a knickerbocker suit and standing 2ft 8in high, an 18 year old youth was yesterday marched into Eastbourne as a military absentee. His escort, who had brought him from Crowborough was a tall Canadian soldier, and the contrast between the pair caused much amusement."

DAD'S ARMY

Most people are very familiar with the Home Guard or "Dad's Army" of World War Two. Far fewer people are aware that a similar organisation existed in World War One. Known as the Volunteer Training Corps (VTC) - it was intended as a part-time local voluntary defence organisation for men over age for the army. Unlike the Home Guard of the Second World War, which came about by official sanction, the VTC was a spontaneous phenomenon. Neither the Government nor the military were keen on the bands of unofficial armed civilians that sprang up as part of this movement. Eventually some order and central control was brought about, and they received official recognition. However, it is interesting to note that early in the war volunteer units were forbidden by the War Office from wearing khaki uniforms, to ensure that their members were not mistaken for members of the regular armed forces. Most VTC units therefore usually affected grey or green coloured uniforms - this is not widely known today, as surviving photographs of VTC men in uniform are naturally in black and white.

Crowborough was at the forefront of the VTC movement, thanks in no small part to the efforts of Sir Arthur Conan Doyle. Sir Arthur played an important role, both locally and nationally, in the development of the volunteer movement. Resisting all entreaties to become an officer in the VTC, he served enthusiastically in the local Crowborough

ABOVE: A Naval recruiting card issued by the Naval Recruiting Office, Nursery Road, Tunbridge Wells. In Crowborough, which didn't have a peacetime recruiting office, local solicitor Allen Hardwicke opened a recruiting office in the High Street and became the town's honorary recruiting officer. Hardwicke's "Scheme for Honorary Recruiting Officers" was apparently adopted by other towns

TOP RIGHT: Sussex Volunteer Training Corps shoulder badge

BOTTOM RIGHT: Sussex Volunteer Training Corps cap badge

LEFT: Allen Hardwicke, local solicitor and Crowborough's honorary recruiting officer

BELOW: Jack Lambert, local raconteur and character poses with a soldier. That the soldier is an experienced veteran is evidenced by his two wound stripes on his lower left sleeve and his four overseas service chevrons on his lower right sleeve, suggesting that he served overseas for four years during the war

TOP: Could this be Private Sir Arthur Conan Doyle standing outside the Red Cross Hotel in his volunteer uniform? Sir Arthur cut an avuncular figure in wartime Crowborough. Across the street a soldier is looking in the window of Southons - to the left of this shop is Barclays Bank (then called Barclay & Co,), and to the right is the then home of the Constitutional Club

contingent as Private Sir Arthur Conan Doyle.

By April 1915 the Crowborough VTC, with its headquarters at the Badminton Hall, at The Croft, had about 40 men in its ranks. *The Courier* reported that; "The members of the VTC wore for the first time in public their new uniforms", and that; "the smart appearance of the dress was the subject of much favourable comment." Over the coming months, partly due to these "smart new uniforms" numbers swelled, and surrounding villages also formed contingents, inspired by Crowborough's lead.

In July 1915, Volunteer units were granted official recognition as bona fide military units, and in August 1916 the War Office included them in the county infantry regiment system and they became numbered volunteer battalions in their local county regiment. Sir Arthur was tireless in promoting the Volunteers. For instance, *The Courier* reported at the end of April 1915 that he gave a lecture in aid of funds for buying rifles for his unit - one of the many fund raising activities he undertook for war related causes during those years. By the latter part of the war the Crowborough volunteer company had some 100 men in its ranks.

YMCA

The YMCA had long worked with soldiers, and a group of YMCA volunteers would often pitch up tent adjacent to the pre-war Territorial Force's summer camps. During the war itself, the YMCA maintained two huts at Crowborough. There was a massive YMCA hut at the Warren Camp, plus another, the Waterloo hut, in the town, which stood on the site of the current Town Hall. These establishments were designed to provide suitable entertainment, such as lectures, musicals and theatrical productions, for off-duty

ABOVE: A postcard showing the YMCA hut at Crowborough Camp - this was opened in March 1915 by Princess Alexander of Teck - a granddaughter of Queen Victoria. It was able to accommodate nearly 2000 men. It had a shop and a stage and provided entertainment and refreshments for the troops based at the camp. There was also a smaller YMCA hut in the town itself (The Waterloo hut), on the site of the present Town Hall. Remarkably a short film clip of the opening of the hut at the Camp by the Princess can be seen on the British Pathe web site (www.britishpathe.com/video/comforts-for-tommy)

LEFT: Soldiers lining up outside the YMCA hut at Crowborough Camp for a concert

LEFT Especially distinguished visitors to Crowborough Camp enjoyed a red carpet and guard of honour welcome

Views From Crowborough

LEFT The Camp's YMCA hut featured in this 'lift the flap' card sent by an unknown soldier Will to his sweetheart Emily in October 1917

soldiers, as well as places they could go to read, write letters or get a snack and a cup of tea.

Whilst the Warren Camp YMCA hut concentrated on entertaining soldiers based at the Camp itself, the Waterloo hut was intended to focus on the smaller numbers of troops based in the town. In December 1915, *The Courier* reported that; "the men attached to The Limes and Lea House (two large houses requisitioned by the army) are to be entertained to tea at the Waterloo hut on Christmas day by Mr Fraser, the popular warden of the hut." Some 120 NCO's (non-commissioned officers) and men from The Limes (Army Service Corps headquarters) and Lea (Leigh) House (Divisional headquarters), plus, rather mysteriously; "the orderlies from Warren Wood" were duly entertained, and provided with presents of tobacco and chocolate from funds raised by local residents.

As well as being a very well used building during the war, the Waterloo hut remained for some years after the end of the war, and continued to serve as a popular civilian venue for concerts, dances and other social events.

LEFT: Inside the YMCA hut at Crowborough Camp. Soldiers seem to have liked to pop in when off duty for a mug of tea and a sandwich or a cake. They were more scathing about the quality of the shows laid on, many of which were said to have been rather staid musical recitals - many preferred to travel to Tunbridge Wells instead to see a variety show at the Hippodrome if they got the chance. According the *The Courier*, the hut was destroyed by fire in January 1917. However two billiard tables and a grand piano were "got out of the premises in time". It must have been rebuilt quite quickly - by March there was a report of a boxing contest held in the "spacious YMCA recreation hut."

RIGHT: As well as playing host to concerts given by civilian artistes, the YMCA huts also provided an opportunity for military personnel with theatrical interests to express themselves, like this group of Royal Field Artillery men

ABOVE: A concert party inside the Waterloo hut given by a Pierrot troupe. Pierrot shows were hugely popular during the war

RIGHT: The YMCA Waterloo hut which stood on the site of today's Town Hall. The homesick soldier who sent this card to his mother in Leicestershire has written on the reverse; "Just sending you a view of the YMCA hut in the village. I am just having my supper in it... I wish I was having my supper at home (even) if it was only dried bread... hoping to get home soon for good, your loving son Clarence."

ARMISTICE

When the Armistice was signed in 1918 the British Army numbered nearly 3.8 million men, and the process of demobilisation soon got underway. Within 12 months the size of the army had been reduced to less than 900,000 and by 1922 to pre-war levels. As this was an Armistice and not an actual surrender by the Germans, most soldiers returning to civilian life were transferred to the army reserve - in theory the war could have started up again and the authorities wanted to be able to re-expand the army rapidly if that happened by recalling men to the colours.

The majority of returning Crowborough men seem to have been successfully reintegrated into the local economy on their return between early and mid-1919. A number of local men who had been made prisoners by the Germans were also repatriated at this time - most of them having distressing accounts to tell of their treatment whilst POW's.

RUSSIAN RELIEF

Crowborough Camp's war was not quite over in 1919 however. In April that year, a special force was assembled at the Camp. The force contained many veterans of the fighting in France and Flanders. These men had been earmarked to be part of the British Army's North Russian Relief Force, put together to extricate Allied forces fighting the Bolsheviks.

In early May the men were inspected by General Sir Henry Rawlinson. According to *The Courier*; "The Russian bound troops included several V.C.'s (Victoria Cross winners) and a number of other men who had won (bravery) decorations in the war." The presence of so many highly decorated men in its ranks confirms that it was a hand picked unit of crack troops. Rawlinson had been involved in many of the significant battles of World War One, and at one time had commanded an Army of half a million

ABOVE: Peace Day 19th July 1919 - the war did not officially end in November 1918, that was effectively a ceasefire. Crowborough joins the national celebrations when the war is finally over in 1919

ABOVE: Comrades of the Great War lapel badge - a branch of the comrades was opened in Crowborough after the war. The Comrades became part of the Royal British Legion in the early 1920s

LEFT: This rare photo, taken by Stickells in early 1919, shows elite personnel of the North Russian Relief Force, which gathered at Crowborough Camp prior to departure overseas in May 1919. The men in this photo, who were volunteers, appear to be combat hardened veterans. Several men wear wound stripes on their lower left sleeve, some have more than one, and at least two of the men have three wound stripes - indicating three separate combat woundings. Two of the officers are wearing Military Cross ribbons for bravery, and a number of men are wearing 1914 or 1914-15 Star ribbons indicating they were early war volunteers or regulars. The man on the extreme right front row sitting down would appear to be a lucky man - he is wearing a 1914 or 1914-15 star ribbon above his left breast pocket and appears to have a number of service chevrons on his lower right sleeve (one chevron was issued for service overseas during each year of the war denoting service in 1914, 1915, 1916, 1917 & 1918 making a maximum number of five chevrons that could be earnt) yet he has come through with no wound stripes on his lower left sleeve. On their lower left sleeve several men are wearing good conduct chevrons. All the men wear the special white Polar Star formation badge of the North Russian Relief Force on their upper right and left arms. All these badges and ribbons would enable a senior officer to judge the calibre and experience of a group of soldiers instantly. Despite their tough appearance, one man is showing a softer side - the man on the far left, sitting, second row, has a tiny kitten on his lap

men on the Somme front. It was to him the Government turned to organise the North Russian Relief Force.

On Monday 12th May, the men proceeded to Crowborough station where they entrained for Newcastle-Upon-Tyne, via London. From Newcastle they set sail for Archangel, Northern Russia on their challenging task - the force finally returned to England in early October 1919.

Meanwhile, the end of the war saw several huts of various sizes from the camp dismantled and sold off. Some were bought locally and evolved into useful residential and commercial buildings.

WELCOME HOME

Also in May 1919 a local branch of the Comrades of the Great War was inaugurated. At a "well attended meeting" some 100 members were enrolled. The Comrades of the Great War was one of several ex-servicemen's organisations formed at the tail end of the war. Eventually most of these organisations came together to form the Royal British Legion.

In June 1919 a Welcome Home Committee was formed in Crowborough to organise a fitting event to mark the men's return. It was decided to hold this in August, and well over 400 local veterans attended the event, which included food, entertainment and "smokes".

Peace Day celebrations in July 1919 included a children's procession from Chapel Green in the afternoon. In the evening a fancy dress carnival and procession. On "Peace Sunday" thanksgiving services were held at all the Crowborough churches, and, in the evening, an open air multi-denominational service was held on Chapel Green. At this, the Rev Akroyd of All Saints expressed the hope; "that the people of the district would never forget what they owed to all the men who had fought for them." St Johns School had its own open air thanksgiving service in mid-July as well.

ABOVE: This photo shows some of the procession that was part of Crowborough's Peace Day celebrations held on 9th July 1919

OPPOSITE: Remembrance day 1924 - veterans assemble at the Cross and prepare to march to the War Memorial to honour the nearly 200 Crowborough men who fell. The two wreath bearers leading the parade both appear to be wearing Distinguished Conduct Medals (DCMs) for bravery, in addition to their campaign medals, likely making them Albert Bailey and George Wickens. The DCM ranked immediately below the Victoria Cross. Most Crowborough men were issued with their campaign medals during 1921-22

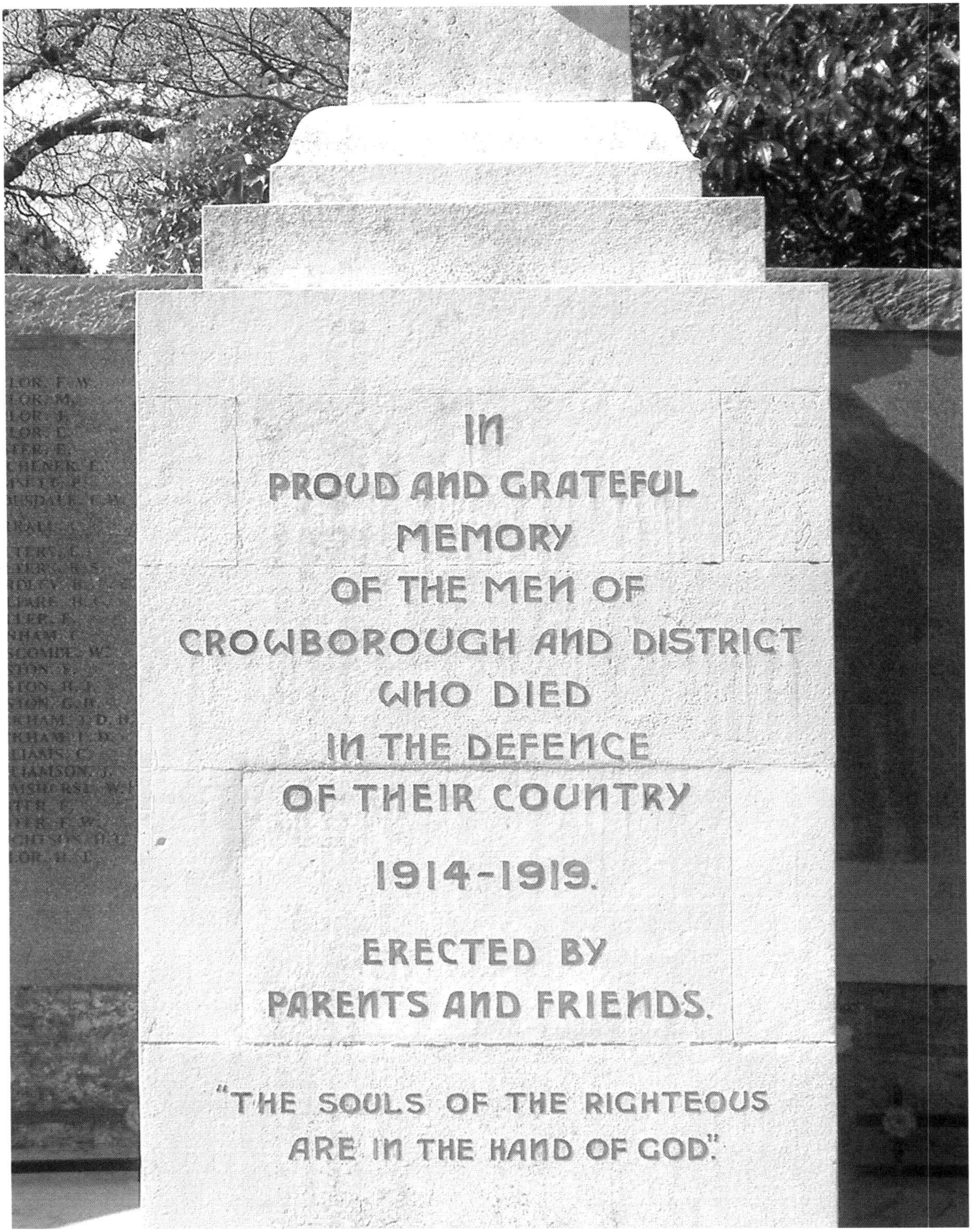
IN
PROUD AND GRATEFUL
MEMORY
OF THE MEN OF
CROWBOROUGH AND DISTRICT
WHO DIED
IN THE DEFENCE
OF THEIR COUNTRY
1914-1919.
ERECTED BY
PARENTS AND FRIENDS.
"THE SOULS OF THE RIGHTEOUS
ARE IN THE HAND OF GOD."

WAR MEMORIAL

Early in 1919 fund raising had started for the War Memorial, and over a period of a few months the donations flowed in. They varied from sixpences donated by local school children to sums of £100-£200 donated by Crowborough's wealthier residents. Frank Humphry, local solicitor and Captain of the Fire Brigade, donated £50. A sum of £489 was donated by the 9th Crowborough Platoon of the 5th Volunteer Battalion - this was the successor unit to the Volunteer Training Corps, after the Volunteers had received official recognition. Sir Arthur Conan Doyle would have been a member, so it's likely he would have contributed towards this total in what in today's money values would have amounted to a tidy sum. The War Memorial was officially "unveiled" on 15th August 1920. The balance of the funds, some £1000, was used to purchase the freehold interest of Preston Lodge, the site of Crowborough's cottage hospital in Southview Road, thus laying the basis for its subsequent expansion and improvement.

CAMPAIGN & BRAVERY MEDALS

Most men who served qualified for the campaign medals that were issued after the war.

Unlike Second World War campaign medals, the First World War ones, which were issued to mark a man's participation in the war, were issued named (a great boon to researchers and family historians). The naming includes the recipient's name, rank, number and their regiment or corps engraved on the reverse or the rim of the medal. Producing these individually named medals was a major undertaking, as several million men had passed through the armed forces, and most men didn't receive their awards until the early 1920's. In addition, several local men won bravery awards during the conflict, including Distinguished Conduct Medals and Military Medals, which were

OPPOSITE: When the war ended the British Empire had lost nearly one million men killed and over two million wounded. Of those that had seen active service, one in five would not return and nearly half would be injured in some way

ABOVE: St Johns school children celebrate the end of the war

issued during or shortly after the war.

One of Crowborough's Distinguished Conduct Medal winners was Lance Sergeant W. G. Wickens. The Distinguished Conduct Medal (DCM) ranked immediately below the Victoria Cross for bravery (and the Military Medal immediately below the DCM). Lance Sergeant Wickens had joined the Sussex Yeomanry in June 1915. He went to France in September 1916 and served there with the Royal West Surrey Regiment's 10th Battalion on the Somme front. His battalion was sent to Italy to help bolster the Italian Army during late 1917 to early 1918, before returning to France. Here Lance Sergeant Wickens was gassed during the last German offensive of the war. His DCM was issued for various actions he undertook during 1917-1918. His citation reads; "For gallantry in action, and continuous good service, and devotion to duty. During the last two years...(he)

ABOVE: Crowborough celebrated Peace Day with a carnival style procession in the Summer of 1919

LEFT: The Distinguished Conduct Medal (DCM) was ranked immediately below the Victoria Cross as an award for bravery. Some four men are thought to have been awarded a DCM out of the 1,000 or more men from the Crowborough area who it is estimated served between 1914-1918

has shown great gallantry and disregard of danger..." Several other men, like Oscar Mackellow, were mentioned in dispatches for efforts above and beyond the call of duty.

THE FALLEN

As well as their campaign medals, next of kin of men who died received a heavy circular bronze plaque with their son or husband's name individually cast on it. This was known colloquially as the "Dead Man's Penny". Special commercially-produced frames were available to buy to mount the plaque in, and many post war homes of fallen men contained what were, effectively, small shrines to the family's son(s) or husband.

Some 193 names appear on **Crowborough's War Memorial** for World War One One of the first Crowborough serviceman to die in the war was Charles Wenham, Stoker 1st Class on HMS Pathfinder. His ship was sunk off St Abbs Head on Saturday 4th September 1914 by the German submarine U21 commanded by Leutnant Otto Hersing. The ship was struck in a magazine which exploded causing the ship to sink within minutes with the loss of over 250 crew - there were only a handful of survivors. Stoker Wenham's widow, Eva, lived at Rose Cottage, Mardens Hill.

One of the last to die, just over two weeks before the Armistice was signed, was 18 year old David Hemsley, who was killed in October 1918 whilst serving with the 7th Battalion of the Buffs (the East Kent Regiment), his parents lived at Sunnyside, Poundfield. For these men's families, and for those of the scores of **other Crowborough men who died**, the war really did mean, as Conan Doyle had predicted in its first few days, that things would, "never be the same again."

ABOVE: The War Memorial as originally configured with the First World War names on both sides of the obelisk. Subsequently they were all moved to the left of the obelisk to accommodate the Second World War names on the right

E. R. DE MORNEY SERVED AS
549 SAPPER
D. J. DOWNEY
CANADIAN ENGINEERS
25TH JANUARY 1917 AGE 27
MICHIGAN

OPPOSITE: D. J. Downey's headstone. D.J. Downey's real name was F. R. De Morney, an American from Detroit, Michigan, USA

LEFT: Sapper Robert Watson's headstone - he died tragically at the mill pond

BELOW: First Class Air Mechanic A J Coleman of the Fledgling Royal Air Force (RAF) - the RAF was only formed in 1918. Arthur Coleman served with its 75th Squadron. The RAF Muster Roll, compiled in April 1918, shows his trade as motor transport driver. He joined the Royal Flying Corps (RFC) as a volunteer on 11 December 1915 at a daily wage of four shillings. His RFC service record seems to be one of the thousands lost in the Blitz, but his brief RAF record does survive in the National Archives. The 75th Squadron records have not survived, but the squadron is thought to have been engaged in home defence duties in southern England between 1916-1918

HERNE CEMETERY

The cemetery at Herne Road (known as Cemetery Road at the time of the First World War) was opened by the parish council during 1905. It contains over a dozen graves of First World War service personnel, British and Canadian, plus that of an American, F. R. De Morney, who served under the alias of D. J. Downey in the Canadian Engineers. All these men would likely have died locally. There are some memorials to local men interred overseas, mostly on their parents' graves.

The gravestones include that of Sapper Robert Watson of the Canadian Engineers who drowned at the mill pond. Crowborough men who died in a war zone would have been buried near to where they fell. It is said that there were only a handful of body repatriations during the whole of the war - all of officers and all occurring before the practice was banned from mid-1915.

The ban was put in place due to the logistical, health and morale problems that would have been associated with the return of thousands of bodies to this country.

ABOVE: All battalions of the Royal Sussex Regiment wore the Garter Star and Roussillon plume badge, except the locally-recruited 5th (Cinque Ports) Battalion, which featured the Arms of the Cinque Ports

ABOVE RIGHT: Stickells' shop & studio in Croft Road. Stickells has left us an important visual record of wartime Crowborough through his photographic images of people and places

AMBROSE STICKELLS

No book on the history of Crowborough During the First World War would be complete without reference to Ambrose Stickells. Ambrose Henry Bensley Stickells, to give him his full name, was Crowborough's premier resident professional photographer during the war years. From 1914, when he photographed the eager young new recruits at his portrait studio in Croft Road, to 1919, when he took his equipment to Crowborough Camp to photograph the members of the North Russian Relief Force, who were gathering there prior to going overseas, Ambrose Stickells tirelessly recorded images of people and places.

Ambrose Stickells was the son of a professional photographer who followed in his father's footsteps. Having initially worked for his father, he set up on his own and moved to crowborough in the late 1890's. At this time Crowborough was a rapidly growing town with no resident professional photographer, the nearest being at Tunbridge Wells.

Initially he worked from a mobile horse drawn photographer's van. When he decided to settle in Crowborough he rented a cottage at Crowborough Cross and parked his mobile workshop in an adjacent field. By the early 1900's Ambrose Stickells had opened a picture framing shop and photographic studio in Croft Road, which still carries a stone tablet with his initials on and the date of the building's completion - 1902. This shop was to be his base for the next 36 years.

For a period of some 40 years in all Ambrose Stickells was Crowborough's chief photographer. Consequently we owe not all, but certainly a great deal, of today's photographic history of the town to his work. With the passage of time many of his photographs have gone on to become familiar images of Crowborough's past.

RIGHT: Ambrose Stickells - crowborough's foremost photographer during the war years

ACKNOWLEDGEMENTS

I am very appreciative of the valuable help and assistance provided by the following individuals in the research and production of this book.

Helen Adams, Terry Bishop, Dr Stephen Davies (Canadian Letters & Images Project), Peter Elliott (Head of Archives, Royal Air Force Museum), John Hackworth, Philippa Hewes (Crowborough Town Council), Tom Humphrey, Lesley Huppert, Dr Claire Isaac, Sue Light (Scarlet Finders), Sue Norton, Pam Plummer, F Robinson, Rita Wilmshurst.

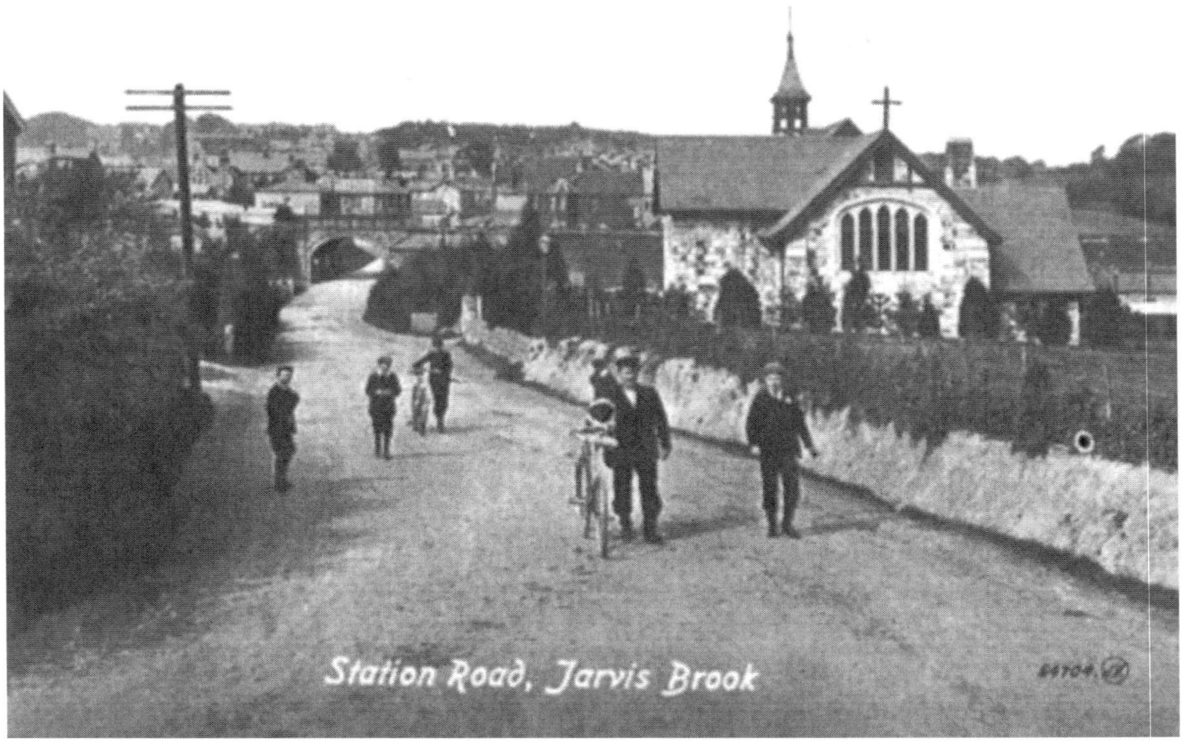

INDEX

INDEX

INDEX

ROLL OF HONOUR

Roll of Honour from Crowborough War Memorial

Adams S
Arnold C
Awcock A
Awcock W V
Bailey F E
Baker W
Baldock C
Baldock S
Baldwin T E
Barnes O
Bartup G A
Beard A
Beard L G
Bennett W
Berry E
Berwick W R
Bishop A J
Blyth H G
Blackford B
Boarer C
Boarer W
Booker H
Booker J
Booker J W
Bolton W
Bridger F
Brooman A
Brooman J
Brown E J

Buck J
Buick L R
Buick R
Bull H G
Camfield G W
Care S J N
Carr W
Causley F
Chaplin J W
Charlton F
Cheesman J
Colbran G
Coleman A J
Cordy-Simpson R
Cornford S J
Cornford T
Cowley H
Cramp A S
Crittall J
Cruickshank A H P
Dadswell G
Dadswell J
Doyle A A K C
Drage C J
Dray A
Dray R
Eyre S H R
Faircloth H
Forward J

Fossey W
French E J
Fry E
Fuller G
Gallard J E
Gander E
Gander P
Gilbert J E
Goble G
Goble H
Goodacre A
Goodacre F W
Goldsmith J
Goldsmith W C
Griffin R Watson
Harman A
Hazelden M
Heasman J
Heasman W
Hemsley D
Hemsley J S
Hemsley L J
Hemsley S H
Henshaw H
Henshaw H
Henshaw W
Hill A
Hill H
Hoadley W J

Hoare M
Hoath A S
Hoath F J
Hoath R L
Hobbs A
Hobbs F
Hodges G W
Hodges J E
Hodges S J
Holden V
Holmwood C W
Hyder F
Hyder J H
Izzard J F
Jarrett A
Jarrett E
Jeffery H W
Jennings C A
Jennings F
Job E D
Jones B
Kingsbury D
Latter W
Leckie M
Ledbitter H P C F
Leslie M
Lester H
Luxford P
Mackellow C

ROLL OF HONOUR

Roll of Honour from Crowborough War Memorial

Maclean A K
May C
Middlemiss G
Middlemiss G W
Middleton F A
Miller F
Monckton O
Moore A
Morley A
Neve A
Neve A E
Norton F
Onslow A G
Onslow B W
Onslow M R B
Ovenden F
Ovenden H
Ovenden W
Page-Mitchell S
Paine C J
Pitt W D
Pollington J R
Pollington O W
Pratt B R
Price H
Ralph W W
Ransom A F
Ransom W A
Randel F D

Richards E G
Riddles P
Ridley E
Ridley V
Ridley W C V
Saunders W K
Shepherd E J
Simmons T
Sivers J
Smith C
Smith S N
Smith W
Southon J
Southon W
Squires W R
Stephens G
Stevenson J
Strange A J H
Sweetman A
Sweetman E
Taylor E
Taylor F W
Taylor H J
Taylor J
Taylor M
Tester E
Titchener E
Tomsett P
Trousdale C W

Verrall C
Walters E
Walters R S
Wardley B
Welfare H C
Weller F
Wenham C
Wescombe W
Weston F
Weston G H
Weston H J
Wickham J D D
Wickham L D
Williams C
Williamson J
Wilmhurst W L
Winter F
Winter F W
Wrightson H T

RESEARCHING A SOLDIER

The main problem to be confronted when researching a World War One soldier is that over 60% of the service records of those who served were destroyed or damaged in an air raid in World War Two. Of those records that do survive, some are incomplete, or suffer from burn or water damage.

Surviving records can be searched online via the Ancestry website (a subscription is payable, but the site often has a free introductory offer period) or at the National Archives at Kew by personal visit – you should ensure you are familiar with their ID and other requirements before you go.

Start your research by examining any war-related possessions or ephemera you may have for your serviceman. His campaign medals will have his service number, rank, initials, surname and regiment or corps engraved on them – armed with this information, a search of the surviving records is much easier.

If you are lucky enough to find a complete service record has survived for your serviceman, this could be full of detail, including his postings and units served with and details of promotions or wounds. Any punishments administered will be recorded on his company conduct sheet.

If you can't find a service record, you can search the medal index cards online at either the National Archives or on Ancestry – it costs a few pounds to download a black & white copy of the medal index card from the National Archives website. The versions on ancestry are clearer and in colour, and can be accessed as part of a subscription to the site.

The medal index cards were intended to show the medal "engraver" what details to engrave on a man's medals – over five million medal index cards were produced. However, if a man's service was entirely within the UK he won't have a medal index card, as he won't have had an entitlement to any campaign medals.

Generally, the cards do not show much information over and above the man's name, rank and number and the units he served overseas with, but occasionally they will be annotated with additional useful information.

Over 800,000 Silver War Badge roll entries are available on the Ancestry website for men who were discharged due to wounds or illness, and these can be searched as part of an Ancestry subscription.

The Kent & Sussex Courier newspaper is a very useful resource for anyone studying a local World War One ancestor – copies of the paper are on microfiche at the Tunbridge Wells reference library. As well as carrying details and photographs of casualties, the paper liked to run features on families with several sons serving, which often includes photographs and interesting details about the men's service. At the end of the war, they reported on returning prisoners of war, often including the returning men's photographs. You'll need a great deal of stamina and concentration to go through all the issues from 1914-1919 in one sitting, so you may like to break this down into two or three sessions.

If you have any clear photographs of your man in uniform, the uniform detail can reveal interesting information. Cap and collar badges can tell you what unit a man served in; wound stripes and overseas service chevrons can also add to your knowledge of the man's war service. If you are unsure what a badge means The Great War Forum online is a great place to ask the numerous researchers and amateur historians with an interest in First World War matters for advice – there are some incredibly knowledgeable individuals who post on the site, and many are very happy to respond to questions posted and to share their knowledge.

If your ancestor died in the war, then the Commonwealth War Graves Commission has a searchable online database, which includes the man's name, rank and number, date of death and place of burial or commemoration. Sometimes useful additional information is included, such as family details or the man's battalion number. Ancestry also has details from the 80 volumes of *Soldiers Died in the Great War*, originally published in 1921, as a searchable database on its site, and it is usually possible to tell from these volumes where a serviceman was born, lived and enlisted.

Regimental museums can also be a useful source of information. Regimental museums vary a great deal in to what extent they are able to handle research enquiries from the public – they can be poorly resourced or rely on volunteers, and may take a long time to reply or make a charge, or ask for a donation, so bear that in mind if you contact one. However, sometimes they can yield very useful information.

Many regiments or their individual battalions produced histories after the war. These sometimes include nominal roles and other interesting information – for instance, the history of the Sussex Yeomanry 1914-1919 contains a nominal roll of all men who served in the unit during the war years, along with details of theatres they served in if they went overseas.

If you have exhausted all these possibilities, and you are still keen to find out more information, it may be worth contacting an independent researcher (the National Archives maintains a list) and running the information you have discovered past them to see if they can recommend any further avenues of research. If they suggest work at the National Archives, it might be less daunting, and more cost effective, to get them to quote for doing the research for you. They will know their way around the archives, be able to quickly locate the relevant records (which they can copy for you) and save you the time and travelling costs of going to Kew yourself.

The National Archives telephone number is: 020 8876 3444

LEFT: 2nd Lieutenant T R Kirby 6th East Surrey Regiment, Crowborough Camp, 1916